# A MEMOIR
# Life for Rent

## WENDY MORRIS

First published by Ultimate World Publishing 2025
Copyright © 2025 Wendy Morris

ISBN

Paperback: 978-1-923255-69-2
Ebook: 978-1-923255-70-8

Wendy Morris has asserted her rights under the Copyright, Designs and Patents Act 1988 to be identified as the author of this work. The information in this book is based on the author's experiences and opinions. The publisher specifically disclaims responsibility for any adverse consequences which may result from use of the information contained herein. Permission to use information has been sought by the author. Any breaches will be rectified in further editions of the book.

All rights reserved. No part of this publication may be reproduced, stored in or introduced into a retrieval system, or transmitted in any form, or by any means (electronic, mechanical, photocopying, recording or otherwise) without the prior written permission of the author. Any person who does any unauthorised act in relation to this publication may be liable to criminal prosecution and civil claims for damages. Enquiries should be made through the publisher.

**Cover illustrator:** Alexandra Nea
**Cover design:** Ultimate World Publishing
**Layout and typesetting:** Ultimate World Publishing
**Editor:** Alex Floyd-Douglass

Ultimate World Publishing
Diamond Creek,
Victoria Australia 3089
www.writeabook.com.au

*For my parents,
for everything*

# Author's Note

This book is a work of nonfiction based on my personal experiences, memories and interpretation of events. While I have made every effort to present these matters truthfully, they reflect my perspective and recollection, which may differ from how others remember them.

For privacy and confidentiality, I have deliberately changed, omitted or obscured some names, places, locations and incidents, as well as the identifying features of certain characters in this memoir. The stories and opinions shared in this book are my own and are not intended to malign, defame or harm any individual, group or entity.

# Contents

|    | Playlist |     |
|----|----------|-----|
|    | Introduction | 1 |
| 1  | Bang Crash Concussed | 5 |
| 2  | The Humblest of Origins | 11 |
| 3  | A Bleak House | 19 |
| 4  | The Game Changer | 33 |
| 5  | The Gap Year | 45 |
| 6  | From Surrey to Mayfair | 51 |
| 7  | Inn on the Park, London | 63 |
| 8  | Dangerous Liaisons | 79 |
| 9  | Cape Town, South Africa | 87 |
| 10 | An Idyllic Greek Island | 97 |
| 11 | Shattered Dreams | 117 |
| 12 | A Death in the Family | 129 |
| 13 | Reinvention | 137 |
| 14 | Secrets Shared in San Pedro | 147 |
| 15 | Magic Tragic Melbourne | 163 |
| 16 | Lizard Island | 177 |
| 17 | Siem Reap, Cambodia | 201 |
| 18 | Resurrection in Sydney | 213 |
| 19 | Did You Know? | 225 |
| 20 | Checking Out | 239 |
|    | Afterword | 247 |
|    | Acknowledgements | 255 |

# *Playlist*

During the writing of this memoir, music from my past evoked memories of particular times, people and places. This led me to include a playlist which accompanies my story. One or two songs which particularly resonated with me as I wrote about certain parts of my life are included at the end of most chapters.

The full playlist can be accessed on Spotify by searching: **Wendy Morris Playlist from her memoir 'Life for Rent'**

The songs and their relevant chapters are as follows:

| | | |
|---|---|---|
| Track 1 | Introduction | *'Life for Rent'* by Dido |
| Track 2 | Chapter 3 | *'Paint It, Black'* by The Rolling Stones |
| Track 3 | Chapter 4 | *'Your Song'* by Elton John |
| Track 4 | Chapter 5 | *'I Thought I Was a Child'* by Jackson Browne |
| Track 5 | Chapter 5 | *'Thunder Road'* by Bruce Springsteen |
| Track 6 | Chapter 6 | *'Hotel California'* by Eagles |
| Track 7 | Chapter 7 | *'In The Air Tonight'* by Phil Collins |
| Track 8 | Chapter 7 | *'I've Seen That Face Before'* by Grace Jones |
| Track 9 | Chapter 8 | *'The Weakness In Me'* by Joan Armatrading |

| | | |
|---|---|---|
| Track 10 | Chapter 9 | 'Running With The Night' by Lionel Richie |
| Track 11 | Chapter 10 | 'So Far Away' by Dire Straits |
| Track 12 | Chapter 10 | 'I Wanna Dance with Somebody' by Whitney Houston |
| Track 13 | Chapter 11 | 'You Were Meant For Me' by Jewel |
| Track 14 | Chapter 12 | 'Oh, Pretty Woman' by Roy Orbison |
| Track 15 | Chapter 14 | 'Honky Tonk Women' by The Rolling Stones |
| Track 16 | Chapter 14 | 'The Closest Thing to Crazy' by Katie Melua |
| Track 17 | Chapter 15 | 'Rise' by Gabrielle |
| Track 18 | Chapter 15 | 'Amazing' by George Michael |
| Track 19 | Chapter 16 | 'Mystify' by INXS |
| Track 20 | Chapter 16 | 'Planets of the Universe – Demo' by Fleetwood Mac |
| Track 21 | Chapter 18 | 'Feel' by Robbie Williams |
| Track 22 | Chapter 18 | 'Army of Me' by Anastacia |
| Track 23 | Chapter 19 | 'Islands in the Stream' by Dolly Parton and Kenny Rogers |
| Track 24 | Chapter 20 | 'mad woman' by Taylor Swift |
| Track 25 | Afterword | 'marjorie' by Taylor Swift |

# Introduction

Over a decade ago, I began contemplating the idea of recounting my life story and even penned a few chapters at that time. Upon revisiting my initial writings, it became evident that I was not ready then to tackle the entirety of my history.

In 2011, as I began the recovery from a tumultuous period that had left me grappling with feelings of depression, anxiety and even thoughts of suicide, my narrative would have likely centred heavily on a brief yet intense phase, failing to capture the breadth of the generally fulfilling life I have led. This focus would inevitably have revolved around the mental health challenges that had plagued me for a few years, making the writing process a daunting task and potentially a less engaging read for others.

While I will address that period in due course, it represents only a fraction of my days. I do not intend to trivialise those experiences but, as I sit at my laptop now, I am inclined to weave a narrative that encompasses not only the hardships but also the delightful and amusing moments that have dotted my years, accepting that one cannot fully appreciate the good times without enduring a few setbacks along the way.

## Life for Rent

Another reason why I believe now to be a more opportune time to embark on this writing journey is that I possess the mental space and time to approach it thoughtfully. After a lifetime marked by constant movement – in terms of homes, jobs, locations and relationships – I have come to the realisation more recently of the need to seek a place that embodies a sense of permanence, even a forever home. I believe I may have found that place.

Instead of feeling compelled to write amidst a demanding 50 to 60-hour workweek, thereby turning it into another chore, I have looked forward to the moments spent reminiscing and documenting my memories.

In the past, I had a massive issue with ageing, to the extent that I did not want to be around beyond the age of 60. Seriously.

However, having surpassed that milestone and now at 67, I have chosen to embrace life, experiencing a gradual shift in perspective over the past few years. I love how I spend my time these days and eagerly anticipate the days that lie ahead.

I believe most of us have compelling stories to tell that often go untold due to various reasons. Privacy concerns undoubtedly play a significant part, a sentiment I can readily relate to. The apprehension of acknowledging regrets and vulnerabilities or re-opening old wounds may also serve as a deterrent for many.

While most of my acquaintances perceive me as a confident and accomplished woman who is well educated, has travelled extensively and been successful professionally, this public persona starkly contrasts with the private insecurities that have played out in my head for years.

A psychologist not so long ago told me that we had made great progress in addressing these issues but suggested delving

## Introduction

even deeper to work through my feelings of shame. I was not ready to go there at the time. I do however believe that I have confronted my problems related to shame within the following pages and the process has been deeply cathartic.

A persistent challenge I have faced is the sense of not being good enough.

I was born into a working-class household in rural England. There were no lawyers, doctors, teachers or entrepreneurs in my family. There were no journalists either, despite my initial aspiration to pursue a career in journalism and become a Foreign Correspondent one day. That dream did not come to fruition.

With memories of the past continuing to haunt me, I realised that writing my memoirs was something I needed to have a crack at. And perhaps, I might be good enough to realise that particular dream.

Encouragement from close friends, who view my life as interesting albeit unconventional, nudged me towards sharing my story for others to read.

So, strap yourselves in for the ride ahead – adventures that traverse several countries with humorous stories and some of the taxing situations encountered during my career in hotel management, as well as delving into the complexities of a dysfunctional family.

And the title, *'Life for Rent'*? Its origin lies in the profound impact that certain songs hold in triggering memories and how they can take us back to a particular time and place.

At the end of most chapters, I've included one or two songs that instantly transport me to that part of my history. I consider

## Life for Rent

myself fortunate to have grown up during the dynamic era of the 1960s and 1970s, a time when the music scene was incredibly vibrant. The ongoing evolution of music has remained of significant interest to me ever since.

This link between my book and the music, which has resonated for one reason or another over the decades, prompted me to contemplate naming my memoirs after a song.

One artist who holds a special place in my heart is the British singer Dido. Her second album released in 2003 was called *'Life for Rent'* and the title track of this collection has always felt very personal to me – particularly its opening lyrics referencing time spent on the move and the absence of somewhere to call home.

*Playlist Track 1: 'Life for Rent'*

# 1

## Bang Crash Concussed

My earliest childhood memory involves accidentally knocking myself unconscious when I was around four years old. I recall climbing on to the seat of the outside toilet (our only one) to reach the old-fashion cistern's high chain.

Despite my efforts to stretch, I couldn't quite reach it. As I extended myself further, I suddenly slipped and fell, hitting my head on the back wall of the toilet. I was out cold and regained consciousness with the doctor attending to me on the sofa in our living room. Apparently, I had been unconscious for some time.

Today, I would have probably been taken to hospital for a myriad of tests, but in the early 1960s, once I woke up and with no broken bones, it was deemed sufficient for me to remain under family supervision. The doctor advised that should I start vomiting within the next 24 hours, I was to be taken to hospital immediately. Fortunately, I did not get sick.

Life resumed as normal – except there was to be no more climbing on the toilet seat and I was to refrain from using the flush until tall enough. Oh God, how embarrassing, that was going to be *years* away!

This probably explains why I had chronic constipation when I was young as I likely tried to avoid the embarrassment of having my every 'movement' monitored. Mum was always dosing me up with laxatives, but I remained stubbornly irregular. But that's enough about my toilet troubles for the opening chapter.

The reason for this story was not only to reflect on my first memory, which could have been my last, but also to indicate that I was a somewhat accident-prone child. Hence, I was regularly nursing minor wounds from stumbling over any small obstacle, falling out of trees I was attempting to climb, tripping into fishponds, boating lakes and other bodies of water… and so on.

Only a week or so after the toilet incident, I decided to help Mum with the ironing and managed to drop the hot iron on my hand causing a nasty burn which took weeks to heal. The extended healing time of the wound was probably due to the copious amounts of butter slathered on it by my mother which was regarded as the cure for superficial burns in those days.

At school, I had a couple of accidents within a short space of time which led nurses at the local emergency department to comment, *'Not you, again?!'*

But more about that later.

On a more serious note, there were two major traumas during my childhood which affected me emotionally for a very long time. The first of these was buried so deeply that I never addressed it until well into my 40s. The other, which took place when I was seven years old, was the murder-suicide involving a family who lived nearby. It happened on 23 March 1965; a date I'll never forget.

The first I knew that something very out of the ordinary had occurred in our small country town neighbourhood was when I arrived home from school to see police cars everywhere. There was a great deal of activity in the street with authorities conducting door to door interviews. However, what alarmed me most was my mother sitting at our kitchen table being questioned by two detectives.

Mum was a key witness, being the first person on the scene of a crime discovered that morning and had raised the alarm that all was not well in the house of her friend. She had popped round mid-morning to have a cup of tea with Helen, who lived with her husband Bill and their only child Mandy.

When my mother arrived, she thought it strange that the milk had not been taken in, back door was locked, curtains were still drawn and there was no response when she rang the doorbell. My mother went straight to Mabel, who was another neighbour, to voice her concerns.

They returned to the house together and decided to investigate further. Unbelievably, they climbed through the kitchen window where everything inside was quiet and the door from the kitchen to living room closed.

As soon as Mabel opened the door, she saw something that made her immediately recoil and say they needed to get more help. The go-to place was the local car repair shop because it had one of the few telephones in the neighbourhood. The owner made his way back to the house and checked all the rooms before ominously declaring, *'We need to call the police!'*

He informed the two women that it looked like Helen and Mandy had been strangled. There was no sign of Bill.

When the detectives left, my mother, who was understandably very shaken, shared the events of that fateful day with the rest of the family. All living together at the time were my parents, 13-year-old sister, maternal grandmother, her 15-year-old daughter (my mother's half-sister) and me.

Discussions continued until late in the day as to what could possibly have happened, and there was little doubt in anyone's mind that Bill had committed the murders. But why, and what had potentially snapped in him? He was a quiet, hard-working, unassuming kind of a guy and, on the surface, the family seemed tight knit and happy enough.

My father, who could sometimes make exceedingly inappropriate comments, said that Bill was *'completely hen-pecked'* (an unfortunate term used back then) and *'There's only so much of that any man can take.'*

Hmmm… Let's move on.

The whole neighbourhood was on high alert that night, fearing there was a killer on the loose.

This fear subsided when the body of Bill was washed up the following day in the local river. There was a collective sigh of relief from the residents in our street. The cause of death was determined as suicide and, following further investigations, that Bill was responsible for the murder of his wife and daughter.

Mum had been a close friend of Helen's and I'd been playing with Mandy on the final evening of her life.

I was seriously disturbed by this incident and for some time, thereafter, would only go to bed if my mother stayed with me until I fell asleep, and a light always had to be left on. To this day, I cannot sleep in the dark. I could never bring myself to walk past the house where the tragedy took place, terrified of the ghosts I imagined lay within. The property remained empty for years.

There was no counselling provided to anyone following the tragedy. We were all just expected to get on with our lives as though nothing unusual had happened. My mother never really spoke about the traumatic experience again, but it must have had an impact on her mental wellbeing. I later learned that this was not the first, nor indeed would it be the last, distressing event she had dealt with alone.

But let's not get ahead of ourselves. First, I should go back in time to briefly trace my parents' background and how they met.

# 2

## *The Humblest of Origins*

My father was born in April 1928 and raised on a small farm in a rural area of eastern England.

Frank was the younger son of John and Susie. He had a brother, Walter, who was six years older. His parents married in 1922, John being 43 and somewhat older than Susie who was just 21 at the time.

John tragically died nine years later; hence the young Frank would hardly have known his father. Despite the age difference, it appears that John and Susie had a happy marriage. Dad always referred to John as a *'good man'*, which I'm assuming was based on his mother's comments since he would have been too young to remember.

It must have been incredibly tough on Susie who was only 30 when John died. Not only did she have to deal with the loss of her husband, but also had two young sons to support, as well as having to run the farm on her own at a time when there would have been little in the way of modern conveniences to make life easier.

At some point, Albert Biggs appeared on the scene and became part of the family when he and Susie married. Albert was seven years *younger* than Susie, and apparently not a very nice man at all. Dad always described his mother as a strong woman and told me how much I reminded him of her. It does make me wonder why Susie was attracted to someone who was so volatile but no doubt her choices at the time would have been limited.

The couple frequently argued and, when Susie wouldn't back down, the arguments escalated into physical abuse from Albert, which extended to his stepsons.

My father was always reluctant to talk about his childhood and I think it must have been even more miserable than he ever revealed. One of the memories he did share was how much he looked forward to Christmas. All that made it special for him was an orange and a sugar mouse. He said that the orange was enjoyed early in the day and then he played with the white mouse until it had turned grey from the amount of handling. And only then did he eat it! My father's vivid recollection of these modest Christmas Day indulgences makes me wonder how stark his upbringing must have been throughout the rest of the year.

Dad also spoke of a younger sibling, who was born to Susie and Albert, and how fond he was of her. He would reminisce about the games they played together before his half-sister died from scarlet fever. Janet was born in March 1937 which meant Frank was already nine years old by then, so a significant age difference.

## The Humblest of Origins

As part of the family history research I conducted for this book, I wanted to establish exactly how old Janet was when she died. I checked the registration of death records but couldn't find anything within the timeframe that had been indicated by Dad in his recollections. Then I decided to start working further back and eventually found the death recorded... In June 1937.

Little Janet was only three months old when she passed away. I've never been able to work out why my father spoke about the closeness he had with his half-sister in the way he did as she only lived for such a short time, and there's no likelihood they would have ever played together as she was a frail infant. Strange.

The tragic loss of their young baby may well have been instrumental in the breakdown of the parents' relationship and for increasing resentment Albert felt toward his stepsons.

As a young man, Walter began to retaliate against Albert, who was only 14 years his senior, and this caused even less harmony at home. As soon as he was old enough, Walter joined the Merchant Navy and never returned to the family. Dad and he remained only in tenuous touch for the rest of their lives and were not close.

With Walter gone, it left a much younger Frank and his mother to deal with Albert. My father helped with labouring on the smallholding, but he also took solace in books reading anything he could lay his hands on. His teachers reported that Frank was an intelligent pupil who had the potential to achieve a university education.

Unfortunately, that was not ever going to happen as he was needed on the farm and, in time, was required to provide care for his ailing mother after she contracted a disease which left her paralysed and in a wheelchair. Despite being only a teenager himself, Dad was Susie's primary carer for several years until his mother died when she was only 46.

The final injustice was when Albert kicked Dad out of the house and took over the farm as his own when Susie passed away which, as her next-of-kin, he was entitled to. I doubt whether there was much desire on Dad's part to stay there anyway. He once told me that at the time, he wished to have died with his mother. Poor man, he must have been completely broken.

So, on a freezing winter's night, the barely 20-year-old Frank left home with only the clothes on his back, a small case with a few bits and pieces inside, ten-shillings (£0.50) in his pocket and walked 12-or-so miles to the nearest town.

The owner of a hotel took pity on the young man and allowed him to stay for a few nights. In an interesting turn of fate, I worked for this same hotelier, who still owned the property many years later, when I began my career in hotel management.

No stranger to hard labour on the land, Dad quickly found employment and continued the back breaking work he had been doing for years. He endured the early starts and late finishes as well as bicycling many miles between the various farms where he worked. At least the bike was a step up from walking, I guess!

My father's unhappy childhood and the financial insecurity which dominated his early adult years led to anxiety which would negatively impact him for his whole life. He was never frivolous with money and always trying to put something aside for a rainy day. It was all about work with my father and he seldom participated in any kind of socialising.

## The Humblest of Origins

As time progressed, Frank managed to put his life back together and wound up moving into lodgings with my mother's aunt and uncle. And that's how my parents met.

My mother was born in November 1931. Jean was the only child of Jim and Nell and was raised in a different house on the same street where I also grew up.

There were a few similarities to my parents' early life in that Nell (like Susie) was pregnant when she married, and Jim (like John) was killed in an accident early in the marriage. Both were young when they lost their fathers and also had half-sisters called Janet. Crazy, right?

Nell went back to work after her husband died and the young Jean was taken care of by Jim's mother, who was always referred to as 'Gran' by the family. By all accounts, Gran was very strict. Nell worked at a local factory which was a five-minute walk from the rented house in Fortune Street. I've always had a little chuckle about the name of that street where we all lived at different times in one house or another, as it was anything but a 'fortunate' address.

A few years after Jim's death, Nell married his brother Charlie. Oh well, I suppose at least she didn't have to get used to a whole new family with her second husband… Charlie was conscripted into the army as the Second World War was underway, so saw little of his new wife.

In 1944, Nell gave birth to a son Mel, and I always believed Charlie was the father but discovered much later in life that this was not the case.

Nell never revealed the identity of Mel's biological father who was noted as 'unknown' on the birth certificate. I wonder how

Charlie reacted when he returned after the war! Regardless of this unplanned addition to the family, Charlie and Nell remained together and had a daughter in 1949 who they named Janet.

This merging of family, with three kids born to different fathers, resulted in some unhappy dynamics. Mum had little in common with her younger half-siblings as there was virtually a whole generational gap between her and them. Even though Mel moved out of home to live with relations when he was a teenager because of ongoing clashes with Charlie, Jean remained much closer to him than with Janet throughout her life. When I learned more about my mother after her death, I understood why she gravitated toward males in the family.

Given that my mother was seemingly such a social butterfly, it's no surprise that school and education held little appeal for her. To be fair though, there would have been no role models in the family to encourage her for anything but a relatively menial job and to get out into the workforce as early as possible. Jean was around 14 when she joined her mother on the canning lines of a local factory.

Now that she was earning a wage, and even though most would have been used to help support the family, Jean had some pocket money for clothes and entertainment. She enjoyed a couple of port-and-lemons on a Saturday night along with a few dances at the local entertainment venue, *The Corn Exchange.*

My parents grew into attractive young adults and romance was soon in the air after they met. Unfortunately, their relationship intensified too quickly when my mother found herself pregnant. After much debating about what to do, where to live and how to support a child, a hasty shotgun registry office wedding was arranged, with little in the way of celebration.

## *The Humblest of Origins*

I don't recall seeing any photographs of my parent's wedding so can only assume that no-one regarded it as a particularly joyous occasion that deserved to be recorded for posterity.

My parents gave birth to their first daughter in September 1951. Mother was only 19 and Father 23 years old at the time. So young!

Not only were they both very young, but my parents were polar opposites in temperament and interests. Mum was friendly, sociable and generally easy-going whereas Dad was suspicious of people, argumentative and decidedly unsociable. My mother was fastidious about her clothes and appearance whereas Dad couldn't care less about the way he looked. The difference between them though which caused most issues and frequent arguments, was that Mum liked to spend money she usually didn't have and often found herself having to deal with household debts, while Dad was super careful and saved his money to the point of being a miser.

I know that plenty of opposites attract and spend a lifetime together happily. My parents did work things out, after a fashion, but it was touch and go sometimes.

I think Dad would have been quite devastated by the responsibility of fatherhood at such an early age. I'm convinced he had dreams of a better life despite his tough upbringing. By the time of Mum's pregnancy, Dad had been working for several years and had acquired an HGV (Heavy Goods Vehicle) Licence, so he was driving all over the country and earning a more generous wage than when he was working on the land. I often wonder had he not become a parent so young whether he might have enrolled in night school to complete his education or saved money to start his own business. He was bright enough and hardworking enough to make a success of himself.

Instead, he continued truck driving for the rest of his life. And to be honest, he loved, as he described it, *'the freedom of the road'*. And without doubt, the solitary life of a driver also appealed to him!

The unplanned pregnancy and marriage meant there was the question of where my parents and their impending child were going to live. Dad was still in lodgings and Mum was in a small house which was already stretched with her mother and stepfather plus two siblings.

An added complication was that Dad didn't get on particularly well with Nell or Charlie. It must have been so stressful as they didn't have enough money to put down a deposit for a house or even rent their own place. Rental properties were few and far between after the war and were also relatively expensive which is why extended families often lived together in cramped conditions.

My parents were lucky enough to be offered a council 'prefab', one of many prefabricated dwellings being rapidly built to deal with the post-war housing shortage and baby boom. It was not luxurious, but the little single-storey property provided a pleasant enough home for the young family which, being newly built, was also neat and clean. Dad later told me that those days in the prefab were some of his happiest.

Almost six years after the birth of my sister, I was born in April 1957.

# 3

## A Bleak House

The relationship between Charlie and Nell unravelled over time and they parted ways. This resulted in my family moving to my grandmother's home in Fortune Street since she could not afford to pay the rent there on her own. The move created another fractious union between different strands of the family. Nell's daughter Janet was around 11 years old at the time and her other daughter Jean (my mother) was by then almost 30 with a husband and two children of her own. But there we all were, six of us in a small, overcrowded property.

Dad took control of the household; however, he didn't get on particularly well with his mother-in-law, and their discord was exacerbated by Nell feeling beholden to my father for keeping a roof over her head. This would have irked my grandmother intensely as she was a stubborn woman who, for years, refused to give Charlie a divorce and his freedom to re-marry, even though she never wanted him back.

As previously mentioned, the house had no inside toilet – everyone had to 'go out the back'. There was also no hot water system which meant heating a kettle on the stove for most of our needs and when larger amounts of water were required for baths and on laundry day, a gas boiler was stoked up in the kitchen.

The only heating in the house was from a coal fire in the living room which my mother would make up each morning at the crack of dawn so that the rest of the family had some degree of comfort when they rose. We would all take turns washing in the kitchen usually, as the bathroom upstairs was just too brutally cold most of the time, and then we would get dressed in front of the fire in the living room. No wonder I sought out warmer climates in which to live when I was older.

There was no refrigerator or telephone, but we did have a small black and white television which all of us would crowd around of an evening in the only warm room of the house, dreading the time when we had to go to bed because it meant facing the Siberian cold of the out-back toilet. The upstairs bedrooms were also freezing in winter, and it was not unusual for there to be frost on the *inside* of the windows and for our glasses of water to be iced over when we woke up.

The whole property was incredibly damp. We didn't use the front room which could have been utilised as additional living space, but my parents couldn't afford to heat two areas, so the room was seldom used and became very dank with peeling wallpaper. I would retreat to that grim space frequently as a child to play with my dolls and imaginary friends, sometimes just to read and be alone.

In retrospect, the need for solitude and being comfortable in my own company was evident from an early age. I developed a strong sense of independence and a feeling that I was 'different' from the rest of my family. At one point, I was convinced I must have been adopted because I simply didn't fit in with those around me. However, Mum put me straight when she presented me with my birth certificate!

When I started to mix with kids from different backgrounds, I began to realise just how basic my family's home was. I started to feel embarrassed about asking friends round as their houses were invariably more comfortable and even luxurious compared to where I lived.

The one day of the week when I absolutely could not have anyone visit was laundry day. I even wished that I didn't have to be there then as the house looked even less welcoming than usual. The whole kitchen was taken over by a jumble of dirty clothes from the household's numerous residents and the back door had to be kept open as there was much to-ing and fro-ing between inside and outdoors, so it was even colder than usual.

My mother used to pray for good weather on laundry days so that all the washing could be dried outside, otherwise the whole catastrophe had to be hung up on lines erected around the kitchen. This caused water to stream down all the walls due to condensation, which compounded the existing damp conditions inside.

The description of our living conditions may sound grim but there were some positives. We always had plenty of good quality home-cooked meals with fresh ingredients. The only convenience food in those days was fish and chips, but we seldom had 'shop bought' as Mum made her own version from scratch which we all preferred.

The house was also very clean as my mother was a fastidious housekeeper. Beds were always made, and linen changed weekly, the sitting room was vacuumed and dusted daily, and windows were washed inside and out each week.

An enduring memory I have is of Mum perched on the outside ledge of the upstairs bedrooms with a bottle of the vibrant lavender coloured *Windolene* in her hand polishing away every speck of dust. This would often be when I was returning from school, and she had already put in a full day's work at the local factory. Mum never stopped. Someone once asked me if she had any hobbies – no was the answer to that question as there were simply not enough hours in a day.

It was a slower pace of life in the early 1960s. Horses and carts were still being used for milk deliveries and I can recall quite clearly feeding carrots to the milkman's beautiful dray horse. Meat, fish and bread were also delivered to the door on a regular basis. Supermarkets did not exist, but we had a well-supplied grocery store just across the road. Equally close was a bakery where everything was made on premises, and it had the best selection of sweets you can imagine, many that could be purchased for just a penny – which probably helps explain my need for extensive dental work over the years!

Even though the town centre was only a 10-minute walk from Fortune Street, we seldom needed to venture from our neighbourhood for any day-to-day requirements. My mother and grandmother used to go into town every Saturday to get their hair done, visit the market and buy a few items to stock up for the week ahead, but it was nothing like the big supermarket shop of today. I think it was kind of nice to have experienced this simpler way of life as a child.

Another pleasure of my childhood was the enjoyment of having pets as the whole family were animal lovers. We had a corgi who was Dad's pride and joy, so she ruled the roost. Judy could do no wrong even when she bit us, which happened regularly since she was such a snappy little thing.

According to my father, it was always our fault for teasing 'the poor dog', but he was less successful in defending the cantankerous corgi when she started nipping the postman and any others she could terrorise. Delivery people took to announcing themselves from the other side of the back gate and wouldn't enter until Judy was safely locked behind closed doors.

We also had a couple of cats as well as a succession of budgerigars, goldfish and hamsters. The passing of each pet was deeply mourned, none more so than Judy. I think it was the only time I ever saw my father cry. All our pets were ceremoniously buried in the backyard with a cross to mark their graves... Well, maybe not the goldfish, they were flushed down the toilet out-back.

After a suitable period of mourning, the deceased animal was usually replaced, and we nurtured and loved the new addition to our family as we had their predecessor.

While my father instigated many improvements to the house, it was the transformation of the garden which became the greatest source of pride for him. The backyard was very overgrown and in need of some love when we moved in and remained that way for a few years. At some point, Dad decided he was going to give it a makeover.

Every weekend, he would be clearing rubbish, digging up overgrown bushes, weeding and trimming the hedges into shape. Eventually, lawn seed was sown but to Dad's dismay the local bird life quickly swooped and pretty much ate the lot, so he had to start all over again. This time though he laid a fine patchwork covering of string on stakes just above the ground (no easy feat) so that birds could not access the seeds without getting caught in the latticed netting. They quickly worked out that a good feed was not worth their likely entrapment.

Dad's considerable efforts were rewarded with a lush lawn and some colourful flower beds. He was justifiably proud, and we all loved this transformed outdoor area. My grandmother, however, in her somewhat surly manner, remarked that she didn't understand why my father would bother to spend so much time on improving a rental property for the landlord's benefit. But there was method in Dad's madness when he purchased the house a few years later.

My mother also wasn't a great fan of Dad's ever-developing enthusiasm for gardening because it meant that an increasing number of hours each weekend was dedicated to this new passion, making him even less interested in socialising.

Soon after the metamorphosis of the depressing backyard into a lovely garden, legislation was passed forcing owners to provide inside toilets and hot water for their tenanted properties. Yay! Times were indeed changing and, as well as these 'luxurious' additions to the house, there soon followed a refrigerator, an automated washing machine and a colour television. Still no telephone though!

When an opportunity arose in the early 1970s to purchase the house, my father had no hesitation in speaking to the bank about a small loan which he successfully obtained. At last, some 20-odd years after being evicted by his stepfather, my dear Dad owned his own home.

Finally, I think some of his security worries lifted. He and Mum seemed more at ease with each other, and they started to enjoy more extravagant holidays. Just to put that into context... It was now a fortnight in Devon or even 'abroad' to the Channel Islands instead of one week in a caravan on the Norfolk coast. In later years, I used to wish I could have recreated that stage of their life for them as they were very happy times.

Some years before my father could afford to buy the house, he had managed to save enough money to venture into car ownership. The first vehicle was a second-hand unreliable 'boneshaker' which I think Dad spent more time on under the bonnet than behind the steering wheel.

Later, he purchased a brand-new *Vauxhall Viva* which was an incredible accomplishment for him. I can remember my father proudly counting out the £600 required before heading off to the dealership to collect his new car. This was a vast amount of money to him at the time. Mum was also pleased with the new vehicle as Dad wanted to show it off to as many people as possible so would take her out on plenty of excursions which she loved.

It was the mid-1960s by then and my sister Sally and aunt Janet were both teenagers pursuing their own interests which revolved around clothes (especially miniskirts), make-up, records and of course... Boys! They both attended the local comprehensive school where there was little emphasis on higher education, so they followed in the footsteps of most young people and left school as soon as possible to seek employment in local factories and shops.

I never had a good relationship with my sister; hence I didn't miss her when she began to spend less time at home. She used to delight in tormenting me which my mother put down to Sally having enjoyed 'only child' status until she was nearly six years old and resented missing out on the attention when I came along. Whatever the reasons, we diverged more and more as the years passed and I remained closer to Janet throughout life.

My first best friend was a girl who moved into the neighbourhood when we were both around four years old. Her name was Anne, and I introduced myself while riding a tricycle past her house where she was playing in the front garden. We enjoyed lots of outdoor play time together even when the weather was cold and miserable, which was most of the time! When it was unbearable to remain outside, we would retreat indoors to play and dress up with whatever bits and pieces we could find.

A favourite game of ours was 'doctors and nurses' when we would enlist Anne's younger brother to join in – not as the doctor, I hasten to add. Anne or I would take turns in that role, with the other playing nurse. Her brother had to be the patient, and I must say, he was always extremely patient with the overbearing young ladies on the medical team!

I seldom invited Anne to my house as it was not a welcoming environment. There was constant bickering and episodes where one family member wasn't speaking to another. There were regular disagreements between my father and his mother-in-law and/or sister-in-law. My mother also had frequent arguments with her sister and older daughter. Sally and I were constantly at each other. However, the rows I dreaded and found most disturbing were the ones between my parents.

It was usually money they argued about. Neither were drinkers, thank goodness, otherwise their disagreements could have really spiralled out of control.

There is no doubt that my father was controlling but my mother, who was generally easy going, was often belligerent toward her husband for no real reason. Even as a child, I figured out that constantly nagging Dad after he had gone to bed for some much-needed sleep before an early start the next day was not going to end well. He just wanted to be left alone.

But no, up to the bedroom Mum would stomp and berate him for what seemed like hours. It would wind up with Dad threatening to silence Mum should she not back off. And there were times when he followed through on his threats. I could hear the whole altercation going on from downstairs and these regular acts of domestic violence distressed me immensely.

It often seemed like a family at war in our household but fortunately, the situations never became too violent or out of hand. Instead, it was the silent treatment that prevailed. In some cases, whenever there had been a serious row, those involved did not speak to each other for weeks or even months. I was always fearful my parents might divorce, and one incident occurred which I really did think was going to tip them over the edge. And this involved an act of violence, though perhaps not quite in the way one might have expected.

As previously raised, Dad's interest in socialising increased when he bought his new car. Most weekends, to Mum's delight, he would suggest they go somewhere or other. Sally wasn't interested in joining these family outings as she was out and about with Janet, but I was expected to accompany my parents which I found *very* tedious.

We usually went to visit extended family, but sometimes it was friends – Dad's strangely enough, given how few he had. He never took Mum to visit her friends as it would have been way too awkward for him to make conversation with people he didn't know. Mum wasn't particularly outgoing but at least she made an effort and as a result, got along with new acquaintances relatively easily.

Terry and Carol were a couple with whom they had a close friendship and we would spend many a (boring) Saturday night at their house. They were an attractive pair in their late 20s, hence a few years younger than my parents, and Terry worked with my father. Mum and Dad didn't consume much alcohol, and each sat on one drink all night. Terry and Carol had a few more but nothing excessive.

One evening, my ears pricked up from watching television when I heard the discussion turn to 'wife swapping'. They were in fact just chatting about some unbelievable stories in the Sunday tabloids and all seemed quite harmless. However, as the evening wore on, there was definitely an atmosphere building, but I can't recall why exactly. Then, quite suddenly, my mother jumped up and said none too happily, *'Come on Wendy, get your coat on, we're going home.'*

Dad was not making any move to get *his* coat on. This was not good. Mum was obviously in quite a rage as she almost dragged me out of the house, and I assumed we'd be walking that night. I think that was the plan… But not before Mum planted two hefty kicks with her stiletto-healed shoe into the side of Dad's new and beloved *Vauxhall Viva*. I was horrified and begged her to stop.

The street was quiet, so Dad would have heard the attack on his car and that *did* spur him into action to make a move. He didn't make a scene and was ominously quiet on the way home. No one said anything as we all mooched inside the house with miserable faces.

Dad picked up a torch and proceeded to examine every inch of his car and soon found the damage, which I prayed was not too bad. But it was pretty bad. And a monumental argument broke out between my parents which went on for days and then there was no communication at all between them which continued for weeks. During this time, the only conversations they had were around separating. I was beside myself and traumatised by it all.

Eventually, things settled down and Dad lovingly repaired his car. I assured him that you would never know there had been any damage. *'But I know'*, he said.

I'm sure he never forgave Mum. There was a definite absence of socialising after that which was Dad's way of punishing Mum. Terry and Carol were seldom mentioned again, and we never spent any more evenings at their place – which was at least one positive outcome as far as I was concerned!

Visits from Uncle Walter (Dad's brother) and his family were another unfortunate occurrence during my childhood as these were seldom joyful occasions. After leaving the Navy, Walter married Doll and settled in East London. It was yet another shotgun wedding with their daughter being born a few months later.

The family would visit us from time to time, always unannounced which didn't go down at all well with my parents. Dad didn't really enjoy Walter's company for many reasons, but one was that his brother liked a drink. Walter would disappear to the local pub soon after arriving at our house and he would return slightly inebriated for Sunday lunch.

Whilst her brother-in-law was at the pub, Mum would be furiously trying to rustle up enough food for all the extra 'guests' wanting lunch, and Doll did not lift a finger to help. After a few drinks, Walter became even more obnoxious than normal, which would invariably cause an argument between him and Dad. The whole disastrous day usually came to an end with Walter storming out (still under the influence) and jumping onto his motorbike with wife, daughter and out-of-control dog loaded unceremoniously into the sidecar. It was quite a spectacle!

I know that many people grow up in far more dysfunctional environments than mine. However, I was always comparing my family with others who were better off, which made me feel short-changed and ashamed of my background. I constantly fantasised about an imagined life in a nicer house and lied to friends to make my home life sound better. Feeling ashamed of such humble beginnings has been a constant presence in my life.

Before continuing, there are a couple of memories from my childhood I would like to share which played out on the television in our small living room. They were events that also captured worldwide attention.

July 1966. Wembley. England playing in the *FIFA World Cup* final. A day for the ages as it turned out. The streets throughout the country were deserted because everyone was glued to a screen somewhere. What was not to love about it?

England had made it through to the final on home turf against the old archenemy (West) Germany and it was a perfect summer's day. The game had plenty of high drama and with a 2-2 score line after 90 minutes it meant there was going to be the added tension of extra time. There was more than a little contention about the next goal scored, but it was awarded, and England eventually claimed victory winning 4-2.

The Queen was there to complete the honours by presenting the trophy to her national team. Will there ever be a day so celebrated again by English football fans? Probably not, but I live in hope. Whenever England reaches yet another penalty shootout of a major tournament, I always say to myself, *'Surely this time.'*

But not thus far in my lifetime. So, it still makes me smile when I think about experiencing that unforgettable *World Cup* victory almost 60 years ago.

In 1969, the world watched in awe as *Apollo 11* landed on the moon. The mission I remember more vividly though is that of the doomed but ultimately successful *Apollo 13* the following year. There was not a great deal of public interest in this lunar expedition until an explosion on board resulted in the moon landing being aborted and a race against time to bring the three astronauts safely back to Earth.

I'll never forget the immortal words of Captain Jim Lovell, 'Houston, we have a problem.'

I remember looking at that beautiful colour image of the earth from outer space on the front page of all the newspapers with the headline: *'250,000 miles from home'* and Dad saying, *'Those poor bastards, so far away. Earth may have its problems, but it must look like paradise to them right now. I honestly can't see how they will make it back.'*

Days dragged on, but finally the crew fired up for their re-entry into the earth's atmosphere. Would the tiny lunar module, which was never designed for this purpose, be able to withstand the intense heat? It seemed not when radio silence with Mission Control went for much longer than expected. As tens of millions of people around the world collectively held their breath (me included) and began to give up hope, the speck of a parachute was spotted in the sky above the South Pacific.

A few minutes later, *Apollo 13* successfully splashed down. I still get goose bumps thinking about it. When Dad returned from work that evening, I was quite emotional, and he assumed the worst until I informed him of the good news.

*Life for Rent*

*'Well, bugger me!'* was Dad's response.

The 1960s were a transformative period in which to grow up. There was much upheaval and many tragedies. The assassination of JFK was probably the most devastating event of that era, however, the loss of Robert Kennedy a few years later, as well as civil rights leader Martin Luther King, were cataclysmic events too. Playing out on the international stage were the Cuban crisis, Cold War and Vietnam War as well as ongoing conflict in the Middle East and a deeply entrenched apartheid regime in South Africa.

At the same time, it was a period when we saw the rise of the counterculture movement, along with increasing creativity in fashion and music with London at its epicentre. And that brings me to my song for this era which takes me slap bang into the mid-60s and the music we listened to at home on the 'wireless' and 'telly'. Mostly when Dad wasn't there!

The two renowned British bands who blazed onto the scene back then were The Beatles and The Rolling Stones. I was and have remained a much bigger Stones fan, and it's hard to go past their first mega-hit from 1965, '(I Can't Get No) Satisfaction'.

However, it's another single, released the following year, that has always captivated me more. The usual suspects are all sounding fabulous – Jagger, Richards, Watts and Wyman – but it's the sitar playing of Brian Jones that I really love, and which always reminds me so much of growing up in the 1960s.

Playlist Track 2: 'Paint it, Black'

# 4

## The Game Changer

*St Augustine's Infants* was the first school I attended; a short walk from home which my friend Anne and I would usually take together.

I loved school from day one, even the mid-morning milk – which was usually lukewarm during the summer months and partially frozen in winter. The milk was provided free by the government to help boost children's calcium and vitamin intake. However, I think that the alternating warm/frozen offering put many kids off milk for the rest of their lives.

The enthusiasm with which I took to schooling was not lost on my father. Despite being a bright and engaged student himself, he missed out on further education because his parents could not afford it, and they needed his labour on their farm. Dad could see how much I enjoyed classes, and he would spend as much time as possible reinforcing and supplementing what I was learning with extra tuition from him. He drilled me in arithmetic multiplication tables and spelling. Dad encouraged me to read and would happily explain the words I didn't understand and how to pronounce them correctly.

In 1964, it was time to move up to primary school which was further away than *St Augustine's* and my parents bought me a bicycle to travel back and forth. There were few school drops by parents as cars were still quite a luxury, plus many mothers didn't learn to drive and fathers would already be out to work from early in the morning. Hence, children usually made their own way to school, some travelling quite long distances.

None of the kids in those days wore helmets when using their bicycles as there was no legal requirement to do so. Believe it or not, the wearing of helmets even on *motorbikes* was not legally enforced until 1973!

The curriculum at primary school was broader and included history, geography and French, all of which I enjoyed immensely. My father was by now working through atlases with me to identify the nations of the world and their locations as well as highlights of British history, amongst other things. He wasn't too hot on the French though. During our home school tutorials, Dad constantly instilled in me that I could achieve anything I wanted with a good education and hard work. He would often say, *'Don't let anyone ever try and discourage you because you're a girl.'*

In the 1960s, females were generally not encouraged to pursue a serious career path. Attending typing school was considered an acceptable choice for the relatively high achievers. Pursuing professional ambition was regarded as pointless since women would likely give it all up to fulfil their expected calling in life which was marriage and raising a family.

Therefore, I commend my father for broadening my perspective from an early age and making me aware that there were other paths available in life.

Anne also attended the same primary school, and we remained close but made other friends too as the school was much larger than *St Augustine's*.

In the final year, I remember feeling a tad jealous when Anne was selected to be the annual 'May Queen' – unofficially conferred on the prettiest girl in the school. But even I had to admit she was! I soon got over my jealousy when I was made Head Girl, which was awarded to the best all-round student in terms of academic and sporting achievements. Yes, way more important than a pretty face I reckoned. Having said that, Anne was a smart young lady too, however, it was deemed that the May Queen and Head Girl roles could not be granted to the same student. Lucky for me!

My parents were proud of the recognition I received but didn't know quite what to make of their younger daughter. There would be more for them to get their heads around before the end of my primary education.

At the age of 11, children were beginning to think ahead to their secondary school options. The system then was that all pupils were required to sit an exam called the 11-Plus to determine whether they would attend the local comprehensive or the far more highly regarded grammar school which groomed students for a university education.

Children at every primary school in the district sat the scholarship and only a handful of pupils would pass the exam. At my school, there were two who passed. And I was one of them. The other student was not any of my good friends, which I was disappointed and a little nervous about. Would I have to start over again and find new friends at secondary school? A somewhat unsettling prospect for any 11-year-old.

There is no doubt that this was a major turning point in my life. No one from my family had *ever* passed the 11-Plus or whatever exam of the day existed to enter grammar school. My parents were so, so proud but also concerned about the significant expense associated with attending the prestigious school.

Unbelievably, there were no fees, and it was only when older did I appreciate what a great privilege it had been to attend this impressive school for free. Nonetheless, there were strict uniform requirements to be met plus books and regulation sports kits. The extensive list of mandatory clothing and equipment required was daunting.

I felt sorry for my parents and I've no idea how much overtime they worked to earn the extra money for everything that was needed. But, come September, I was kitted out as well as any other pupil at my new school. I was beside myself with joy, pride and anticipation. Aunt Janet shared in my excitement, and she took the time, as mother was at work, to ensure my uniform was correct for the first day of term before sending me off with a big pat on the back.

The *High School for Girls* was a beautiful heritage-listed Regency building overlooking the river. It had been extended over the years to facilitate classrooms, science laboratories and a music wing. The grounds were extensive and allowed for several hockey pitches during the winter and around 20 lawn tennis courts in the summer.

The majority of pupils came from relatively affluent families who were urged by their parents to perform well academically.

## The Game Changer

In some cases, there was considerable pressure placed on students to become high achievers which created quite an air of competition in the classroom and on the sports field.

There was a broad curriculum covering all the standard subjects and a strong emphasis on sports. Many of the girls aspired for selection to the school hockey and tennis teams which competed with schools in the region throughout the year in various championship leagues.

To complete our preparation for tertiary education, which would pave the way for a profession or management career, we also had elocution classes. My father may have been a truck driver and my mother a factory worker, but I was quickly developing a 'posh' voice which belied my humble origins.

Other than maths and art classes, I loved everything about my new school even the large amount of homework. I was not gifted academically unlike some of the other students who breezed through with natural brilliance, but I quickly grasped that by studying hard I could make the grade. So, the pattern began of my putting in extra effort and time to achieve success.

There have been a few periods in my life when I've put personal relationships ahead of education or work, but generally my default position has been to place greater importance on nurturing a successful career. This is not surprising as my father had been impressing on me from an early age that I would have to work hard to do well in life, and his words stuck.

I even recall him saying to me once when I couldn't have been more than 12 years old that he didn't think I would ever marry and for sure never have children. I must have been so intent on fulfilling his prophecy that I can honestly say marriage and children were never really on my radar.

*Life for Rent*

Instead, I developed a fiercely independent nature. Subsequently, even though as an adult I've had several long-term relationships, deep down I never felt any of them would last forever. Hmmm, let's see how that works out in the future…

I threw myself into studying hard in the classroom and practising hard on the playing field. I performed well in all subjects (except art) with even my maths becoming passable. I made it onto the first teams for both hockey and tennis, was elected captain of my class and the sporting teams and took part in debating and French-speaking competitions. I was a regular member of the school dramatic society, as well as the choir where my claim to fame was writing and starring as the matador in the Spanish section of a musical we produced called *'The Lost Chord'*.

It went something like (and *really* cannot believe I still remember this):

> 'Your chord arrived upon the
> evening of the bullfight just last week
> Concealed inside the folds of
> Don Sebastian's cloak so smooth and sleek
> The people gathered in the marketplace
> before the fight began
> Excitement mounted, cheering, screaming,
> every woman, child and man.'

To round things off, I was a regular contributor to the school magazine with poems and articles from school trips.

Phew…no wonder, with all the pressure I was placing on myself to be not only accepted but excel in this new and elite world, I developed an eating disorder when I was around 14 years old which led to a spell in hospital and took years to overcome.

## The Game Changer

My concerns about leaving friends from primary school when I passed the 11-Plus exam became redundant when one special friendship blossomed shortly after I started high school. And has endured to this day.

My dear friend Deborah, who is still as beautiful on the inside as she is on the outside, lived in a magnificent property called *Broadlawns* that overlooked the school grounds.

Deborah was tall and striking, with long legs and a mane of blonde hair, the combination of which was to get her into a fair bit of strife with the boys when we later became a co-ed school. But before all that, as soon as we met in our first-year class, we instantly connected.

Deborah often invited me for a meal or a sleepover and I used to marvel at the size and elegance of her house. I had to reciprocate her invitations at some point, which I was dreading. But this darling girl never batted an eyelid and accepted me, my home and my family for who we were and never made me feel in any way lesser than she.

As we progressed through our teenage years, Deborah began to spend more time at my house as she was often 'in disputes' with her parents who were quite strict whereas mine were relatively easy-going. She even joined us on family holidays a few times and my parents became very fond of her.

School excursions were an important part of our education which included visits to different parts of England to provide practical study for our geography and history curriculum as well as overseas to appreciate different cultures.

The trips were partially subsidised, however some costs had to be paid directly by the student which again stretched my parents, but they didn't want me to miss out. Over three consecutive summers, I was fortunate enough to visit Europe, America and Russia.

Those school excursions exposed me to a broader world and sowed the seeds for a lifelong travel bug. All these new experiences created yet another difference between how I saw my life panning out and my family's general expectations, which were extremely limited as far as I was concerned.

It cannot be overstated how much this school altered the trajectory of my life and made me ambitious to succeed. But I had already set some limitations.

I made the decision to study a subject at university that would lead directly to gainful employment. Further education was going to be another financial burden on my parents, and I owed it to them to get it over with and out into working life as quickly as possible. Hence earlier notions of studying journalism were abandoned as this would have most likely required additional years in a low-paid cadetship.

When the time came for applications to be lodged, I found a university course which fitted the bill perfectly and sounded interesting too. But first, I had to obtain enough O-levels, which are taken at the age of 16, to be able to stay on at school for another two years and study three A-level subjects, which were in turn required to be passed for acceptance on to a degree course.

Despite the influx and distraction of adolescent males into my life at the age of 13 when the boy's grammar school in town merged with the girl's high school, I continued to perform well academically in the lead-up to O-level exams.

## The Game Changer

To be considered for A-levels, students had to pass a minimum of five subjects. I passed all nine of my subjects with good grades, so progression was not an issue. Mum and Dad knew how hard I had studied to do so well and were once again very proud of me.

A couple of years later when I came to sit my A-levels, all of which I needed to pass with reasonable grades to have my university place assured, it was more of a close call. I passed all three subjects, one at a high grade but the other two only just scraped in at the required level. I had been expected to achieve high results in all three subjects but in the second year of study, I found myself enjoying 'other interests' – my first serious boyfriend.

My father was extremely disappointed with my A-level results and didn't let me forget how much the relationship had affected their outcome, even though I still secured university entry. But he got over it. After all, I was the first family member to make it through to any kind of formal tertiary education.

My desire to study a subject at university which would lead directly to paid employment made me opt for a course at the *University of Surrey* in Guildford (just south of London) to complete a four-year Bachelor of Science degree in Hotel and Tourism Management.

As well as training me for a job I could start immediately after graduating, I liked the scope of the course itself. The subjects included Law, Economics and Finance, as well as those which concentrated specifically on hotel management and tourism.

The degree was heavily geared toward developing skills for a future career in hospitality and I was advised when attending the interview that the dropout rate from the course was quite high, but significantly lower for students who had spent time working in the industry prior to embarking on the degree.

I was encouraged to think about this as an option and take a year out before commencing university. I would later discover that the hotel industry with its long and unsocial hours requires great dedication. Therefore, because of the university's recommendation but also, if I'm honest, as my boyfriend was having to take an extra year in school re-sitting some subjects to obtain the grades he needed for university placement, I deferred my entry for 12 months to gain some hands-on exposure to basic hotel operations.

Prior to commencing the next chapter, I should explain the circumstances behind my winding up in the emergency room at hospital *twice* in quick succession while at school.

The first time was the result of a chemistry explosion. Our teacher was quite laid-back and had set up the apparatus to make concentrated sulphuric acid without, it would become apparent, some of the necessary safety precautions. Being a dedicated student, I was sitting in the front row of class so took the brunt of an explosion which resulted in me being covered in the burning chemical.

I remember rather calmly and politely raising my hand saying, *'Please sir, I think it's gone in my eye.'*

A speedy visit to the local hospital ensued where I was patched up and sent home. My father returned from work to find me on the sofa with an eye mask and bandaged from head to foot. He was naturally somewhat concerned but satisfied by my assurances that I was okay.

These days, the school would face serious legal action for negligence but that would never have crossed my parents'

## The Game Changer

minds. I recovered but had numerous burns which took a fair while to heal, and still have the scars.

A week or so later, during the crucial mid-season period, I was keen to return to the hockey field. In my first match back, I attempted to save a certain goal by the opposition and tackled a player from the wrong side (which was a foul) to prevent them from scoring.

This caused my opponent to miss the ball, and her hockey stick came straight into my face at full force. This is why when playing hockey, you should never tackle from the left-hand side! So, back I went to the emergency room again, this time for stitches to a split lip (from which I also still have a scar) prompting the nursing staff to say, *'Not you again!'*

*There are many songs which prompt memories of my high school days and the one I've selected is a single released in 1970 which launched one of the world's most successful artists, currently in his sixth decade on the music scene — the one and only Elton John.*

*Playlist Track 3: 'Your Song'*

# 5

## The Gap Year

My first serious romance was with a young man named Daniel. He was the youngest son of parents who owned a significant amount of agricultural land in the local area.

Their eldest son was already at medical school when I met Daniel. Middle son Tom was less academically inclined and enjoyed an active social life that largely consisted of hanging out in pubs with a succession of girlfriends.

All three boys were educated and boarders at an expensive private school. I often heard snippets about Tom and Daniel who were hotly pursued by many of the local young women because both were good-looking.

In addition to being genetically blessed, they came from a wealthy family. Their large house was in a desirable part of town; the parents took exotic overseas holidays and owned a succession of luxury cars. Hence any of the sons were regarded as a *'good catch'*.

At some point, I can't remember how or when exactly, my best friend Deborah met Tom and they were already in a steady relationship when Daniel returned home from boarding school to complete an extra year of study and improve his grades for university entry.

Daniel was quite shy, and I think oblivious of his good looks. I thought he was well out of my league on every level so didn't pay too much serious attention to him when he joined my class at school, until one night he showed up at a local event I was also attending. We got chatting which led to a dance and then a good night kiss at the end of the evening. Afterwards, we started spending more time together and a romance developed.

At the start of my relationship with Daniel, I had concerns about how he or his parents might react to my family's relatively lowly position. However, neither party showed any sign of being in the least bit bothered by my background. Instead, they embraced and included me in their lives.

Daniel, a genuinely kind and gentle person, was well liked by everyone. My mother particularly adored him and harboured hopes of us getting married in the future. She even grew accustomed to the 'embarrassment' of me getting picked up from our modest home by Daniel's father in his flashy *Aston Martin*. This often drew the attention of nosy neighbours peering through their curtains as the car roared into and out of our street.

Based on remarks directed at my parents – which were variations of, *'Who does she think she is?'* – it was clear that some in the neighbourhood believed I was reaching well beyond my station in life. Oh dear.

It's interesting to reflect on that period when Deborah and I, who shared a close bond akin to sisters were in relationships with the two brothers, but in fact we didn't frequently socialise together. This was largely due to Deborah pursuing her Law degree at *Nottingham University* after finishing school which resulted in Tom travelling back and forth to visit her. Meanwhile, Daniel and I mostly stayed in our hometown during my gap year, so it was seldom all four of us were in the same place.

My 12-month deferral of university was to be used primarily as an opportunity to work in the hotel industry. Before that though, I was awarded a sponsorship by the local rotary club after I'd applied to them for a grant to make a study of the Swiss tourist industry. Switzerland had a long history of actively promoting itself as an attractive destination for overseas visitors and tourism was a major economic driver for the country.

The rotary club set up my various accommodation requirements and industry appointments with their member networks in Switzerland. I was basically alone much of the time and all the travel was unaccompanied, which was a first for me, and quite nerve-racking given that I was only 18 and fresh out of school. It provided me with yet another amazing adventure abroad.

Upon my return from Switzerland, I found a job in the picturesque village of Wansford at a charming 17th century coaching inn, now known as *The Haycock Manor Hotel*, an upscale hotel and restaurant. I was provided with on-site accommodation which represented my first move away from living at home. Little did I know then that I was destined for a life on the move and would live in close to 50 different places and five countries before settling where I am now.

I commenced in the entry level position of bartender (then commonly referred to as a 'bar maid') and worked with two fabulous women who were not only glamorous, but smart and funny, too. We had a hoot and despite the long and unsocial hours – working evenings, weekends and public holidays – I found genuine pleasure in the job and especially its customer service element. It didn't take long for me to realise that I had a natural aptitude for hospitality.

And so began my career in an industry which would continue for over 40 years. On reflection, I wonder whether this same path would have been chosen if I had my time over? Probably not is the surprising but honest answer. Despite many memorable times, the demands of hotel management ultimately proved to be very onerous. However, long before there was any disenchantment with my chosen profession, I loved my first job in a hotel.

A few months after starting at *Haycock Manor*, I returned home to see Daniel and attend his brother's 21st birthday which was a big party at the parents' house. I was a serious cook back then and made several rather fancy desserts for the occasion. The next-door-neighbours attended Tom's party, and they were the owners of *The White Lion* which was known as the best hotel in town.

The neighbours were most impressed by my culinary skills and subsequently made me an offer to work in their hotel kitchen. Whilst I was enjoying *Haycock Manor*, I wanted to spend as much time as possible with Daniel before we began university and so accepted the offer.

*The White Lion* was the establishment with its same owners in which my father had been given refuge when he left his family home. Dad never forgot the kindness of the hotel owners who in turn spoke highly of the decent and hard-working young man they had helped all those years ago.

When I first started at *The White Lion* I met with some resistance from the male chefs, not only because I was female but also

## The Gap Year

because I was 'friends' with the owners. However, once I proved myself to be a hard worker, keen to learn and could actually cook, the boys soon settled down and treated me respectfully.

The hotel industry then, unlike today, was *very* male oriented and for years, as I rose into junior and middle management roles, there were few other women. In the 1970s, general managers came predominately from food and beverage backgrounds, which were strictly male domains. It was unusual to find females working in high-end kitchens or restaurants, which meant women were also absent from general management positions.

Later, there was a shift in the industry landscape when the accommodation side of hotel operations began to receive greater acknowledgement. Managers with experience in rooms division became sought-after and since positions in this area were more accessible to females than food and beverage, in time women found themselves increasingly in demand for senior roles.

Eventually, the glass ceiling was shattered, leading to a growing number of women entering positions in general management.

I've encountered few instances of gender prejudice in my career, which is surprising considering how male-dominated hospitality was when I started. I put this down to being incredibly hard working and aspiring to be the best at whatever role I was in at the time. I'm sure my values are in common with many other women who, regardless of their ability and work ethic, have still met with discrimination. So, maybe, I've just been lucky.

I passed a pleasant summer in *The White Lion's* kitchen, living at home again and seeing more of Daniel. Soon enough, October 1976 came around and it was time to take up my deferred entry to university.

## Life for Rent

By then, I had some understanding of hospitality and really enjoyed the work so was looking forward to the next step in becoming a Hotel Manager. Daniel and I had been together in a serious relationship for well over a year and were not too concerned about the changes to come. Our respective universities were not far from each other, so we planned to catch up every weekend. Furthermore, there would be the long university holidays to spend quality time together.

Daniel was very into music and introduced me to the artists he followed. This exposure to new performers in my late teenage years, and the fact there was a great deal around to like in the 1970s, has led me to include two songs for this chapter. Both are from musicians who were relatively unknown back then.

Whenever I see the album cover of Jackson Browne's 'For Everyman', released in 1973, I immediately think of Daniel and the hours we spent listening to this record. My favourite track is included in the playlist.

Playlist Track 4: 'I Thought I Was a Child'

In 1975, Bruce Springsteen's breakthrough album burst into our lives and oh how I loved it, especially since the title track featured a girl named Wendy! The album and single are 'Born To Run'. This is not however the song I've selected – instead it's the opening track of the album with its incredible keyboard backing to the Boss's distinctive vocals.

Playlist Track 5: 'Thunder Road'

# 6

## From Surrey to Mayfair

My father drove me to university in Guildford and its accommodation which was a hall of residence on campus. It was the first of many trips my parents made over the years to visit me, and Dad complained every time about having to navigate the London traffic which he hated.

After we arrived, I was anxious to get myself organised and settled, ready to attend the fresher's orientation that evening, but Dad was reluctant to leave me all alone in my new place. I told him not to worry, everything was going to be okay and that I'd call later – yes, my parents had *finally* installed a telephone! He eventually left for the three-hour drive back home and afterwards, I did indeed feel somewhat solitary in this new environment with no friends or family close by.

However, I soon settled into the routine of lectures, tutorials and assignments as well as life in general on campus. Compared to school there were fewer formal classes, and this required self-discipline to organise my time effectively for independent unsupervised study.

I received a full grant from the government to attend university which was not required to be repaid from future earnings. This provided the opportunity for young people from less affluent backgrounds to gain a tertiary education. I feel very, very fortunate to have benefited from this system. I still worked throughout my time at university though, in various cafes and restaurants around Guildford, as well as in the student union bar a couple of evenings a week.

Daniel and I continued our relationship and saw each other most weekends which worked out for a while. But as the year progressed, both of us made new friends with whom we spent more time overall, and gradually began to have less in common with each other's lives.

Between study, work and spending weekends with Daniel, I didn't have much time to build a network of buddies at university and often felt on the outside of friendships which developed in class. There was only one person with whom I was close, and we remained good friends for several years after completing our degrees. Her name was Jane, and she was a sweet girl from Sunderland with a lovely Geordie accent. She and I shared a flat together in year two of our studies.

During the first semester of my second year in Guildford, I became increasingly fond of someone in class and decided to call time on my relationship with Daniel over the Christmas break. It wasn't a very merry Christmas, as you can imagine.

My new boyfriend was called Harry who was outgoing and sociable. He was also bright academically and did not need to devote long hours to study, whereas I did. As I began to spend more and more time with Harry, my grades went downhill and it came as quite a shock to find myself barely in the top half of class, after previously being one of the higher achievers.

Regardless of declining academic results, I managed to get a placement at one of my preferred London hotels for the third year in the degree course, which was 12 months of work experience, referred to as our 'industrial year'.

I was very excited to land a management trainee role at the five-star *Grosvenor House Hotel* on London's Park Lane. At last, I was going to work in a real luxury hotel with close to 500 rooms and multiple departments. It seemed like a lifetime ago when, years earlier on a Sunday afternoon outing in his new car, Dad had driven into central London and down Park Lane to show me the swanky hotel properties where the rich and famous stayed.

I believe that trip made an impression on me and subconsciously sparked my interest in hotels. However, residing in London and working in Mayfair was not a future I could have imagined as a child. And yet, in 1978 at the age of 21, there I was.

Jane and I continued as flat mates during our year in London and moved to an apartment in Kensington which we also shared with a couple from class who had both elected to work in five-star hotels for their industry placements.

Jane had opted for training with a company specialising in corporate events and her work usually involved regular hours from Monday to Friday. The rest of us, being part of 24/7 hotel operations, were working all sorts of crazy shifts and usually weekends. We used to tease Jane about taking a soft option in the corporate world, but she had a far better work-life balance.

We were lucky that our apartment was so centrally located in London, just a short walk from Kensington High Street with its tube station and numerous bus connections. I doubt whether students would have the luxury of living in such a central location these days as rent would be prohibitive. I can remember taking countless number 73 buses to and from work and being dropped on the doorstep of *Grosvenor House*. I continued to work on Park Lane for several years after I graduated from university and the grandeur of that area in the heart of Mayfair never failed to inspire and excite me.

Harry and I had been together for a year or so by then and our relationship became somewhat long distance when he chose to pursue pub management outside of London for his industrial year. Pubs in the UK were transitioning at that time with franchises popping up around the country offering good quality affordable accommodation and the beginning of the gastro pub concept to compete with traditional restaurants.

An introduction into the rigours of hotel working life came early during my tenure at *Grosvenor House*. One of the first departments for my training was in Room Service and I covered breakfast shifts which started at 6.30am each day.

To earn some extra cash, I offered to work on one of the cocktail parties scheduled to be held in a number of the hotel's private suites for a large conference group which was staying in-house. I assumed that the cocktail party would run for a couple of hours early evening then everyone would head out to dinner, and I would be able to leave soon after. My assumption was incorrect.

Guests had been invited back to the entertainment suites for post-dinner drinks and I was expected to hang around until they returned, then continue to serve drinks and snacks until everyone retired for the night. I didn't get home until after 2.00am and had to be ready to start the breakfast shift again just a few hours later!

This was the first but certainly not the last time I would be handling fast turn arounds at work. I found it relatively easy by perfecting the art of a cat nap almost anywhere I could close my eyes for at least 10 minutes (usually on the tube or bus) thereby reviving my energy quite quickly.

Overall, I loved my year at the hotel but there were some departments I didn't particularly enjoy, namely Housekeeping. My exposure to this area however gave me a lifelong respect for housekeeping staff as the work they do is incredibly hard and generally undervalued. The disappointment of some departments was far outweighed by my enjoyment of Front Office, Human Resources and my time with the Management Accounts team.

I also spent several weeks in the vast kitchens of *Grosvenor House* and apparently was the first female to prepare a dish that was served in their fine dining restaurant, *La Fontaine*. Note, I was not allowed to work in the restaurant itself as it was a male only domain for service!

The Executive Chef did his best to persuade me to give up my aspirations for a career in management saying, 'We could make a bloody good chef out of you!'

I wonder where that might have led but have absolutely no regrets on the decision to stick with management. To succeed as a top chef is unbelievably demanding and the work environment very pressured. It's little wonder that so many chefs have 'issues' – anyone who has worked in hospitality could write a book on that subject alone.

The hotel handled large functions for up to 2,000 people and had an extensive banqueting kitchen which was manned by a different brigade of chefs from those that catered for the restaurants. I completed a stint in banqueting as part of my training too but enjoyed it less than the a la carte kitchen as the work felt more like being on a production line than creating elegant dishes cooked to order for the restaurants.

One funny incident I remember was after a day in the function kitchens when I had been preparing the main course for a large dinner that evening. I had pan-fried literally hundreds of chicken breasts in readiness for the final preparation before service. It was tiring and tedious, processing tray after tray of chicken for most of my eight-hour shift. I was glad to be in the bus on my way home when I finished work.

It was a warm day, and I noticed a rather unpleasant odour, so looked around wondering if there was perhaps a vagrant person close by. No, I couldn't see any such individual. And then I realised to my horror that the smell was emanating from me! Even though I'd changed my clothes after work, the smell of all that fried chicken had made its way on to my skin and into my hair.

I was so embarrassed, as by then I'd noticed a few other people looking around trying to work out who the stinky passenger was. I jumped off the bus near the *Royal Albert Hall* and walked the rest of the way home. Under the shower, it took a great deal of scrubbing and numerous applications of shampoo to get all that oil off my body and out of my hair. Luckily, my turn in the banqueting kitchen ended soon after this episode and I moved on to more pleasant working environments.

## From Surrey to Mayfair

We had a number of celebrities who stayed at *Grosvenor House*. In particular I remember Sean Connery, who was a regular guest when visiting London. One evening, I was working at Concierge alone fiddling around with some paperwork under the desk with which I was pre-occupied and didn't notice our VIP approach. I think Mr Connery had stood there for a while waiting for me to attend to him before I heard, in that unmistakable deep Scottish accent, *'I say, do you think you could possibly hand me my room key please?'*

I jumped up and banged my head (still accident-prone even then!) but quickly recovered to apologise and grab the key from the rack. Throughout my career, I've been pretty good with remembering room numbers, dates and names, and said, 'Certainly, Mr Connery, that would be room so-and-so?'

He gave me a charming smile as I passed him the key to his luxury suite. I glanced over to the reception desk where the supervisor on duty gave me a withering look. It was a timely reminder of never allowing yourself to get distracted with paperwork at the expense of keeping any guest waiting – especially one of the establishment's top VIPs.

After a successful traineeship at *Grosvenor House*, it was time to return to university and complete the final 12 months of my degree. There had already been a few students drop out earlier in the course and more followed after the industrial placement stage when the demands of a life working in hospitality proved too much for them.

I don't recall any second thoughts and wanted to get back to central London in another five-star hotel as soon as I could, but ideally somewhere smaller than *Grosvenor House* and not part of a large chain.

Later that year, the university's annual dinner-dance was held at *Inn on the Park*. The property is now known as the *'Four Seasons London on Park Lane'*. As I swept down the hotel's majestic staircase that evening in my floaty ball gown, I knew that this was where I wanted to work when I graduated.

In the mid-1970s, *Inn on the Park* was the newest luxury property in London. It boasted the most expensive rooms in the city, and probably still does. It was managed by Canadian group, *Four Seasons,* which was relatively unknown at the time. No one could have predicted the phenomenal growth and future influence this company would have throughout the world.

Today, *Four Seasons* has become the epitome of a luxury brand and the benchmark for other hotels to measure themselves against.

I made enquiries with our placement tutors about the possibility of a position with *Inn on the Park* and was told the hotel did not take graduates for management training, therefore should consider another property in which to start my working career.

I was bitterly disappointed, but a few months later, as luck would have it, *Inn on the Park* approached university about enrolling two students on post-graduate programmes, initially as a trial to determine whether they would be interested in a long-term partnership with the hotel department.

I could not believe my good fortune and knew that I had a very good chance for selection. There was one position in Food and Beverage and another in Front Office.

My preference was for the Front Office programme as I had only limited experience in this department to date, but I would have been delighted with either of the traineeships. After several interviews, the Front Office role was offered to me. I was ecstatic, but first, I had to get through my fourth year of study and graduate from university.

The final year was tough with coursework and assignments intensifying in preparation for the last set of exams – all of which carried a higher proportion of overall marks than the previous three years. It was critical to perform well in the last year as it had a big impact on the classification of your final degree.

Harry and I were still together, however his drinking and excessive socialising with a couple of close mates had escalated, which concerned me.

I began to spend more evenings with Jane who was a great support. There were many lonely nights when I was feeling despondent about my relationship with Harry and fearful we were going to break up. I was not eating properly and had lost weight which also happened during my school years when I felt out of control.

This issue would continue to manifest itself throughout life with weight being the barometer of my overall wellbeing. The fluctuations are not huge, but definitely noticeable. The lighter me is usually an indication of something being out of balance in my mental health and the heavier me is usually indicative that I'm in a settled space.

Even more alarming during this time, when really depressed, I started to self-harm by cutting myself with a razor blade. Thankfully, I didn't do too much damage but still have a few scars. This disturbing behaviour had the desired effect supposedly of capturing Harry's attention, and he was genuinely worried. He promised to curb his behaviour and made good on that promise. We became closer as a couple and decided to move in together after graduation.

Yes, we got there in the end and graduated! Despite *all* my hard work and distinct *lack* of study by Harry, we both wound up with the same second-class degrees. University life was over, and we were ready to start our working careers.

In common with most people, I'll never forget my graduation day. Mine took place in June 1980 and my parents drove down to attend the ceremony in Guildford Cathedral, next door to the university campus. They were *extremely* happy. Dad gave me the biggest hug saying that, despite friends telling him what a waste of money it had been to support a daughter through university, he was so incredibly proud of me for having successfully completed my degree.

He laughed and said he couldn't wait to boast about his *'headstrong daughter who now had letters after her name.'*

Indeed, I was now a B.Sc. (Hons), and that was a relatively rare achievement for women at the time. Back then, fewer people enrolled in full-time education after the age of 18 than today, and those that did were predominately male from more affluent backgrounds.

Being female and from a working-class family, I was *very* much in the minority in the late 1970s. My parents were as pleased with me as I was thankful to them for the many sacrifices they made to support my pursuit of a university education.

*There are a few songs that take me back to my student days. The one I've selected is the title track from Eagles iconic album 'Hotel California'* released in 1976, the year I started university. It was sometime before I bought it, however, because much to my annoyance a student who lived below me played the opening song non-stop and very loudly in the first few weeks after the album's release!

Playlist Track 6: 'Hotel California'

# 7

## Inn on the Park, London

It's hard to know where to begin on the three extraordinary years I spent at *Inn on the Park*. I commenced there in July 1980 as a management trainee, before progressing to Assistant Front Office Manager and later to Sales Executive. The quality of the people I worked with throughout my time at *Inn on the Park* and everyone's commitment to exceedingly high standards of service was truly exceptional. My experiences at this iconic property were transformational both personally and professionally. I also made some treasured life-long friends.

My front office management traineeship began on Reception where the check-in area consisted of two beautiful oak tables in the lobby which was an innovation at the time. Instead of standing at a counter to register, our guests would arrive and sit down opposite a member of staff, making it a less formal and more relaxed interaction. Each guest was personally shown to their room by the receptionist and their luggage followed with one of the hotel porters. As you can imagine, for a 200-room property running more than 90% occupancy year-round, there needed to be a large team of staff on hand to facilitate this level of service.

Most of the five-star properties in London had predominately male staff on reception in those days, but *Inn on the Park* had other ideas on this too and their team consisted solely of females. There was also a minimum age in place for the women who worked on reception, which I believe was around 23, to ensure they had a degree of maturity in handling the high-end guests. It probably goes without saying that a 'certain look' was required for a place on the team. It wasn't about being ultra-glamorous, though some of the girls certainly were, as much as being confident and outgoing.

Our uniform was a smart suit and, if working into the evening, a change to long skirt and evening blouse was required. There were strict grooming rules and God forbid should you report for duty looking anything less than immaculate as the reception manager would, in no uncertain terms, order you back to the staff locker room to make the necessary adjustments in your presentation.

I felt that the leader of this feminine enclave was cautious and sceptical of me due to my academic background. Having worked her way up in the industry, the reception manager may have been concerned that I would be ambitiously pursuing advancement and might threaten her position.

However, over time, we developed a strong working relationship and became friendly. This capable woman demonstrated a sound work ethic and was the person you wanted around in a crisis – qualities she seemed to recognise in me, as I eagerly absorbed her guidance and training like a sponge.

## Inn on the Park, London

There was no short supply of crises almost daily as the hotel was *very* busy. The Front Office team worked under considerable pressure to achieve capacity occupancy, and its high-end clientele did not take kindly to being 'bumped' to another property when *Inn on the Park* was overbooked. Yet, we were required to handle these tricky situations on a regular basis.

The upside to running such a robust financial bottom line was that no expense was spared in the presentation of the property and the service provided. There were some lovely touches which were regarded as unique at the time like fresh plants in rooms, the finest Egyptian cotton bed linen, toiletries by *Floris* in the bathrooms, sumptuous bathrobes (for children as well as adults) and exquisite hand-crafted petit fours made by the hotel pastry chefs for all arrival guests.

Our Head Concierge could secure flights, limousines, theatre tickets and all manner of requests no matter how limited the supply might be or the late notice of the request. It all came at a price, of course, but our guests were very generous, and the tips we received were unbelievable.

The guests who stayed at *Inn on the Park* were wealthy individuals, mostly North American businessmen (lots of oil men) and quite a few from the Middle East (more oil men), plus a smattering of celebrities from the film and music industries.

Shortly before I started working there, Howard Hughes had been in residence occupying the whole top floor of the hotel. He was already well into his eccentric lifestyle by then, so was never seen in public and the rooms he occupied were all screened with block-out blinds to ensure no intrusion of camera lenses from the media scrum who were constantly camped around the hotel.

There were many stories of the craziness surrounding Mr Hughes, mostly relating to his extreme obsession with germs and the measures he took to protect himself. I wish I'd been there to witness it all; I did wonder though if perhaps some of the stories were a little exaggerated. Probably not.

When I began working at *Inn on the Park*, its most regular guest was someone else on the global rich list at that time who we referred to as 'The Doctor'.

He had been staying at the hotel regularly for a few years but wanted to maintain a home base in London where he could leave personal belongings and come and go as he pleased while having the full service back up of a luxury hotel. He was renovating a huge apartment in town, but this was taking longer than planned so a rate was negotiated to keep a suite booked for his personal use at the hotel 365 days a year, and to house his numerous cars in the hotel garage.

He was in residence barely 30% of the year and paying today's equivalent of around £1,000 a night to keep the suite available for his use when he dropped into London. It was not unusual for him to come to the desk and hand over up to £50,000 at a time in cash!

There were a few of us who were obviously favourites with The Doctor and he would often ask us out, which we politely refused. When the guest's home was finally completed and he moved out of the hotel, he invited most of the management and front office team to a lavish dinner at *The White Elephant* overlooking the Thames. The venue was an extremely expensive and fashionable restaurant, but no longer exists today. It was an incredible evening, and we all had a lot of fun.

## Inn on the Park, London

Sometime later, I had a dubious encounter with another regular guest. Let's call him Mr Bashir. He was a wealthy businessman from the Middle East, who sometimes stayed at the hotel with his wife. Mr and Mrs Bashir were a very chic and friendly couple who I often checked in and escorted to their room. I remember them being generous tippers.

When travelling alone, Mr Bashir was always pleasant, courteous, and totally appropriate in his interactions, so when he invited me for lunch one day I thought nothing more of it than a friendly gesture.

I arranged to meet him at the *Royal Garden Hotel* in Kensington where he was staying as *Inn on the Park* was fully booked. I was expecting to have lunch in one of the hotel's restaurants, however when I called Mr Bashir's suite, he informed me that he had arranged to have lunch served there instead and would I mind joining him? I was slightly taken aback by his suggestion but thought I was being overly concerned since I had met the man on numerous occasions with never a hint of impropriety on his part.

It began amicably enough when I arrived at his suite. Mr Bashir was smartly dressed as usual, and I started to relax as he poured me a glass of (very good) champagne. He said that lunch had been ordered and wasn't far away, and in the meantime, we made small talk about my career aspirations in hotel management, as well as his business interests and visits to London.

We were sitting at opposite ends of a large sofa but then he started to shuffle nearer and, when close enough, made a move to touch me. I jumped up startled, trying to keep talking as though nothing untoward was happening, and managed to position myself behind the sofa. He continued to follow me while I moved further away, feeling increasingly alarmed. I wished that the room service lunch would arrive soon, so that I could make my get away while there was another person in the room. Then the thought crossed my mind that perhaps there was no lunch on its way, so I decided it was time to visit the bathroom immediately.

As calmly as I could, I excused myself, locked the bathroom door and took a few deep breaths. There were no mobile phones in those days, but all five-star hotels had telephones in their bathrooms. I flushed the toilet and ran the taps to create some background noise. Then, I picked up the telephone and called my good friend Sara who was secretary to the Assistant General Manager at *Inn on the Park*.

She quickly orchestrated a plan for my escape by calling the *Royal Garden* and requesting to be put through to Mr Bashir's suite. Hopefully, the telephone would be picked up and this would cause enough of a distraction for me to get out. Sara said that if the phone was not answered, she would grab a cab and come over to rescue me.

Feeling rather more in control of the situation, I gingerly exited the bathroom, and my host apologised for having made me feel uncomfortable. He sat down on the chair opposite after topping up our champagne glasses. Soon after, on cue, the telephone next to Mr Bashir rang and thankfully he answered it.

I made sure that my handbag was right next to me and plotted the quickest route to the door. He cupped his hand over the telephone receiver and with a confused look on his face, told me that it was a receptionist (Sara) advising that my car had arrived and was waiting on the driveway. I smiled and said, *'Oh yes, must dash, have to get back to the office!'* and dash I most certainly did.

## Inn on the Park, London

I literally ran out of that suite and down the hallway toward the lifts. On the way, a waiter with a large room service trolley was sauntering down the corridor from the opposite direction. The lobster and salads looked delicious and there was more champagne accompanying the lunch. In passing I said, *'I hope he's hungry,'* and received a strange look from the waiter. I made it down to the lobby and with a sigh of relief, jumped into a taxi.

Lesson learned. Trust your gut instincts when faced with a potentially compromising situation and do not accept invitations to meet a man you hardly know in a private location. No harm was done, but afterwards I realised how silly and naive I had been to go to the guest's suite alone. I do not recall Mr Bashir staying at *Inn on the Park* again.

There were several amusing episodes involving celebrities during my tenure at the hotel. One of these involved Sammy Davis Jnr who was booked to stay during some shows he was performing in London. He was another guest who required several rooms set up for his rather unusual lifestyle and nocturnal habits. He liked to have most meals prepared by his own team of staff, so one room had to be cleared for this purpose. He was a night owl who slept for a good part of the day, hence there was a lot of activity around his collection of rooms during the night which meant there could not be any other guests nearby. Numerous bodyguards also ensured that no one ventured close to the Davis accommodation.

On the day of Davis's arrival, a grand piano arrived in the loading dock which everyone assumed was for him even though we had not received any notification of a delivery. However, it wasn't unusual apparently to receive last minute challenges when Sammy was due to arrive. Furniture was hurriedly re-arranged in the sitting room of the main suite to be occupied.

The delivery guys transported the piano to where it need to be situated, and they left.

Soon after, the Front Office Manager received a call from the Mexican embassy who had made a reservation for their President's wife to stay at the hotel for a few days. We learned that she was a keen pianist, and the call was to inform us that a baby grand had been arranged for her stay which would be arriving soon and was to be placed in her suite.

Okay. So, the piano was already on site but in the wrong room. No problem, the transport team just had to come back and relocate it. But unfortunately, they were on the road and engaged with other work until later in the day. As we pondered whether the piano's relocation could wait, our Head of Security advised he had just received a call from one of Sammy's staff to say they were getting into limos at Heathrow Airport and should be arriving at the hotel in about 45 minutes. Great!

The baby grand was a cumbersome and heavy item that required a delivery team of four men with specialised equipment who had been able to use the service lift for its transfer from the loading dock to the suite. It was decided that a few of us should at least attempt to move it ourselves – but the service lift was too far away, and the fire exit was much closer, so that was the route we decided to take.

Using a good deal of brute force, we managed to get it into the hallway. At that point, we received another call to say ETA at the hotel for the Davis entourage was 10 minutes.

It was relatively simple to slide the piano along the hallway, but navigating the fire escape door was quite another thing altogether. Maintenance had to remove the door so that we could get the piano into the fire escape and there we all were breathless and

## *Inn on the Park, London*

sweating when we heard the message come through on the security walkie-talkie that Mr Davis was on his way up.

At this stage, all of us nursing a baby grand would have been clearly visible when the lift opened as we were perched in the exit which was missing its door. Fire escape doors are heavy, and they come off a lot easier than going back on again. So now, as well as trying to keep the piano stable on the stairwell, several of us were holding the door in place to get the screws back in so that it would close.

*Ping.*

That was the sound of the guest lift arriving on our floor.

*'Right, the door's on,'* gasped our maintenance man. But we realised part of the piano was still in the doorway. We all just looked at each other and no words were required – we mustered our collective strength to heave it out the way.

*Click.*

The fire door closed. At that moment, we heard the lift open with our Front Office Manager calmly sweet-talking the legendary Sammy Davis Jnr, welcoming him back to *Inn on the Park*.

In the stairwell, as relief set in, we all started to giggle uncontrollably but still needed to move quickly as Davis's security detail we knew would be checking the fire escapes very soon. The room for the Mexican First Lady was allocated on the floor below, so we only had one set of stairs to negotiate, plus it was downhill, and we managed this relatively easily.

At last, we had this piano where it was supposed to be and it did look quite magnificent, so much so that it was considered to keep it there as a permanent fixture. However, the cost was deemed to be beyond even our hotel's lofty budget. We were also mortified by our relatively rough treatment of this fine musical instrument when we knew how much it was actually worth.

Another entertaining story involved telexing a racy screenplay for two regular guests who were fledgling filmmakers. Before there were even fax machines, telexes were used to send written communications around the world. A *telex* machine was like a huge electric typewriter, requiring a tape to be made for long messages. When completed and ready to send, the paper tape was fed through the machine at an automated speed.

One evening, I was given the scene from a movie which needed to be telexed to the *Golan and Globus* office in New York. The script was for a re-make of *Lady Chatterley's Lover*. The film makers were beginning to make their mark in the industry with several risqué productions, being either sexually explicit and/or violent. The scene I had in my hands fell into the former category.

I was laughing as I typed away which caused one of my colleagues to stop by and take a look for herself at what was so funny. I finished the tape which must have been about a mile long, fed it into the machine for transmission and off it went.

The critics had a field day when the movie was released in 1982 starring Sylvia Kristel. It flopped both critically and at the box office. The company did, however, have later mainstream success with rapidly emerging demand from the made-for-video market, as opposed to movies made for release at the cinema. Even today, whenever I come across a movie listed as a *Golan and Globus* production, I have a little chuckle to myself remembering that telex I sent all those years ago.

## *Inn on the Park, London*

There was also the highly publicised 1980 release of the movie *10*, starring Dudley Moore, Julie Andrews and Bo Derek (in her first major role). In this romantic comedy, the screen newcomer's appearance is described by Moore's character as being a perfect 10-out-of-10. Not sure that such a story line would go down too well today but the film, even though quite silly, was a commercial success.

It became the subject of many dinner party conversations regarding the 'perfect' physical attributes of its star. And not forgetting discussions about who might now be having sex while listening to Ravel's *'Bolera'* – check out the movie to discover that part of the story line!

There was huge press interest in London due to the British stars as well as the stunning young American actress. Bo Derek and her husband stayed at *Inn on the Park* for the movie's release and, as you can imagine, our security team had their work cut out keeping the paparazzi at bay. In person, the actress was indeed beautiful with exquisite facial features. She was very charming and the male staff at the hotel were in their element, falling over themselves to be of service.

I was promoted to Assistant Front Office Manager after about nine months working as a trainee on reception. The role was a newly created position and reflected the need for an additional member on the management team due to the hotel's consistently high levels of business. I worked closely with Front Office Manager Roberto in this position, and we got along well. He excelled in interacting with guests and was familiar with all their preferences. He did however lack strong organisational skills, which is where I had an important function of handling his administration efficiently. I thoroughly enjoyed my new role.

Roberto worked long hours. He had to be on hand to greet late arriving VIPs as well as catch up with clients who were only available in the evening. Roberto would often introduce me to these guests, and one was a man who had been in the secret service for the recently deposed Shah of Iran. I found his stories fascinating and he and I would spend many a late evening chatting over coffee or a few drinks.

After leaving Iran, he set up his own security business in the United States protecting many famous clients. He was obviously doing very well to be able to afford a stay at *Inn on the Park* when he visited London.

A final brush with fame came on my last night as Duty Manager, shortly before leaving the hotel. Duty management involved coverage after hours and handling any issues that may arise when the rest of the senior team were off duty.

On this particular night in July, it was the middle of *Wimbledon*, and London's hotels were choc-o-block. We were as usual overbooked, and I was holding the only decent room in town that I could find as a back-up at *The Savoy*. I was about to finish for the day and hand over to the Night Manager. Despite having worked at the hotel for several years and very competent, he didn't have much experience in bumping guests as everything had usually been sorted by the time he came on duty.

Our last arrivals were off the New York to London *Concorde* flight which arrived at around 10pm. I knew we had a guest who was going to try and catch the flight at the last minute, and we had confirmed the availability of his regular suite. However, there had been a mix-up with the dates and the suite was only in fact available the *following* day.

## Inn on the Park, London

By the time this error had been picked up, every room in the hotel was occupied, hence the reason for the suite I was holding at *The Savoy*. The guest was Chairman of one of the biggest TV networks in America. The Night Manager begged me to stay and deal with the situation. I reasoned that it would all be quite straight forward as the guest may not have made the flight and, even if he did arrive, we had alternate accommodation lined up for his relocation. But I stayed on all the same.

And just as well I did because who did Mr Chairman stroll in with about 20 minutes later? None other than the high-profile son of then British Prime Minister.

I took a deep breath and launched into the 'bump' spiel with humble apologies, etc., etc., but hey good news, *'We'll just pop you into a cab and one of the best suites at The Savoy is booked for you… Okay?'*

Not okay. I think that Mr Chairman was so tired he didn't care too much but still he didn't want to *'Go all the way down the river to The Savoy.'*

His companion then became quite agitated exclaiming, *'This is preposterous!'* and continued for several minutes with his tirade.

I think even Mr Chairman was starting to feel sorry for me by then and said, *'Look, I understand there has been a misunderstanding and that you weren't expecting me until the morning, but I need to stay somewhere closer as I have a heavy schedule tomorrow.'*

*'Alright, let me see what I can do,'* I replied, *'I'll need to make a few calls,'* knowing it was going to be a lot of calls I would most likely have to make and that it was going to be quite futile anyway. I settled both gentleman into the lounge with refreshments and headed back to the office.

But luck was on my side. I called the *Intercontinental* first, since it was literally next door, and one of my good contacts there was on duty, also working late waiting for several guests to check-in from the *Concorde* flight.

As expected, they were fully booked but my contact said she would double check to see whether there had been any last-minute cancellations. After what seemed an eternity, she came back to me with the news that there was a room available since one of their guests had missed the flight. Yay!

When I told Mr Chairman that I'd managed to get him a room at the *Intercontinental*, he was thrilled and keen to get over there as soon as possible. I escorted him on the short walk across Hamilton Place and waited until he had checked in.

By the time I returned to *Inn on the Park*, it was well past midnight.

'*Can I go now please?*' I asked rather cheekily.

The Night Manager smiled and said he'd called a cab to drive me home to Wimbledon (where I lived at the time) on the hotel's account, which I was grateful for as I probably wouldn't have taken that liberty for myself.

'*Thank you so much for staying back. We'll miss you here when you go,*' he said as I left.

The hotel didn't hear anything more on the matter, but I know that our PR Manager was on tenterhooks for a few days. She complained bitterly to Roberto in her most indignant French accent, '*Hooow could this possibly hahppen to one of our top VIPs? It might have turned into a total pooblic relations disaster for the hotel.*'

## Inn on the Park, London

The unflappable Roberto just rolled his eyes and gave her a look that said, *'Settle down, we sorted it!'*

The suite being held at *The Savoy* was never used that night, but we still had to foot the bill which would have been close to the equivalent of £2,500 today. As you can imagine, our Financial Controller had a few choice words to say about that.

I have recounted just a few of the memorable episodes I had while at *Inn on the Park*. This chapter has covered my working life, but significant changes had also taken place on the home front. Professional and personal life merged in this period which influenced my next move…and the rest of my life. These developments require their own chapter.

I was busy and worked long hours at Inn on the Park but tried to keep in touch with the music world. There are two songs which take me back to that era of my life and both are from albums released in 1981 by very different artists.

First is the opening track from the debut solo album by English singer-songwriter Phil Collins, 'Face Value'.

Playlist Track 7: 'In The Air Tonight'

Second is from the unique Grace Jones. I really enjoyed her album 'Nightclubbing' and one of its singles in particular.

Playlist Track 8: 'I've Seen That Face Before'

# 8

## Dangerous Liaisons

After Harry and I left university, we lived in a few different places around London. Initially, we rented a dingy top floor of a converted house in Wimbledon which didn't even have a proper bathroom – the shower cubicle was in the hallway as you walked in the front door – and the property backed on to a railway line, so we had noisy trains shunting back and forth virtually 24 hours a day.

I hated it there and after a few months, started to look for something better to move into. I found a lovely apartment in Pimlico which was *just* within our budget – well, not really, but I managed to persuade Harry that we could afford it from savings we would make on transport expenses, not to mention the convenience of a significantly shorter commute to and from work. Living in Wimbledon added around two hours to our working day, but from Pimlico I could walk to *Inn on the Park* and Harry was nearer his base in Leicester Square, so it meant he would have much easier travel too.

After the dismal accommodation in Wimbledon, it was fantastic to be living in the relative luxury of our new place with the exclusive SW1 postcode and stayed there for about six months. We moved when our friend Alex found an apartment in Bolton Gardens, South Kensington which he asked us to share with him.

This was the same Alex with whom Harry used to have many a wild night at university, so I was concerned to have the two of them living under the same roof. But when I saw the property, I was won over. It was bigger than our place in Pimlico, with an extra room for guests and a lounge area that opened to a lovely private garden.

After moving in, all was well between the three of us to begin with. Alex, who was a nice easy-going guy, had ditched a career in hospitality and moved on to working in the financial services sector. This was the early 80s and at that time, there was a great deal of money to be made from selling investment and private pension plans. Alex was earning so much in commissions that, within a year-or-so after leaving university, he had bought himself a brand-new *BMW*.

He was out-and-about most evenings in fashionable bars and restaurants, returning home late with his new network of friends who were all enjoying quite the hedonistic lifestyle. I didn't like the partying, but as I was usually in bed, it didn't affect me too much – *except* for cleaning up the following day.

Harry was managing restaurants and usually working dinner shifts so was also turning into a night owl and participated in a bit of 'winding down' with Alex and his mates when he arrived home.

I was making new friends at *Inn on the Park* with whom I enjoyed a busy social life after work, however these evenings were usually not late nights since most of us had an early start to our working day. We made the local bars and restaurants of Mayfair our playground.

Consequently, it was hardly surprising that Harry and I began to drift apart. Even though we were living together, we hardly saw each other and very rarely went out as a couple. The after-work drinks which were part of my evenings usually involved some of the hotel's senior chefs whose company I enjoyed. There was a fair amount of flirtatious behaviour, but I remained mindful of my professional standing at the hotel and understood the importance of not overstepping boundaries.

It seemed that I was something of a novelty to the boys due to my relatively senior position at the hotel, the youngest female in a management role and my willingness to socialise outside of work hours. They were also aware of my long term, live-in relationship so refrained from pushing the boundaries...too far.

The disharmony between Harry and I intensified after I met someone from within my broader hotel network in London and with whom I'd felt an immediate connection.

When I first met Peter, I didn't realise he was married. Today we have *Facebook*, *X* (formerly *Twitter*) and *LinkedIn*, to name just a few of the social media platforms which allow us to check out whoever, whenever. It was much easier back in the 80s to keep one's private life just that.

Hence, I was surprised to learn a few weeks after meeting him that Peter had a wife and children. I tried to dispel my disappointment at this unforeseen development but assured myself that it was probably all for the best. I was attracted to Peter, but at the same time, did not wish to become involved with a married man, particularly as I had a long-term partner myself. I determined to brush aside any romantic notions and keep our interactions purely on a platonic basis.

That remained the case for almost a year. Over time though, we became closer. Peter and I both worked late and sometimes caught up for a drink with others from various hotels in the area, but usually most of them were about to head home when we arrived. It was then, when there was just the two of us, that our conversations grew increasingly intimate.

One Saturday night, towards the end of an event which we both attended, Peter asked if I would like a lift afterwards, *'Since your place is on my way.'*

Which was true, sort of. On the drive home, it was obvious that neither of us wanted the evening to end and we wound up going for dinner around the corner from my apartment. And that's when the affair began. I was 24 at the time, considerably younger than Peter, but should have known better. And he certainly should have.

Shortly after, I ended my relationship with Harry and moved out of Bolton Gardens. I relocated to a rental unit in Wimbledon, within a charming small complex. I was so fond of the building and its location that when a small studio there became available to purchase, I decided to buy it. Despite the return to a longer commute, I relished owning my own place.

By then, I was working in the role of Sales Executive, which was a welcome break from the rigours and long hours of operations. My working days consisted of being out-and-about in London visiting clients, in addition to entertaining decision makers in the hotel.

*Inn on the Park* continued to enjoy high room occupancies; therefore, my sales focus was on attracting business for the banqueting department which included product launches, cocktail parties, award dinners and so on. The major international banks frequently organised formal loan signing events, followed by lavish lunches. These functions were highly profitable, and I was tasked with winning as much of this business as possible. I was constantly in the City (London's financial hub) visiting the many institutions based there, most of which were located in very opulent offices.

I was certainly enjoying the high life and having a wonderful time, hosting clients at the hotel virtually every day, as well as attending many grand external events. I remember being invited to the relaunch of the *Orient Express* which was a fabulous trip recreating the classic first leg of the legendary train's European voyage.

Since my professional life was so busy and interesting, it felt quite liberating to be single again. To begin with, the relative uncertainty and spontaneity of the relationship with Peter also worked for me.

As time moved on, Peter confided that his married life was becoming more fractured, which was hardly surprising given the nature of our ongoing affair. His wife knew he was required to work long hours in the management position he held but, after a while, began to have her suspicions about there being more to Peter's prolonged absences than pressure of work alone.

The situation came to a head a year-or-so after Peter and I started seeing each other when an excellent overseas opportunity arose for him.

Peter was very interested in the role, and we discussed the possibility of 'a new beginning' for our relationship in another country. He was quite vague about what the repercussions of this would be for his family...

When I later learned that his wife had accompanied him to the interview abroad (he told me he had travelled alone), it began to dawn on me that for Peter this was indeed a plan to create a new start... Just not with me.

When Peter returned, he resigned from his London employment and left to take up the overseas appointment pretty much immediately.

I was devastated by how our relationship ended so suddenly and decisively. I increased my workload at the hotel and volunteered for more shifts at the restaurant where I moonlighted on evenings and weekends. I would get home late at night exhausted and then bury my sorrows in a few glasses of wine before starting all over again the next day.

I dated a couple of chefs at the hotel who were both great guys, but I wasn't really into either of them because my heart was broken. I felt foolish about what had happened to me which was the typical outcome for 'the other woman' in most affairs. The naivety in allowing myself to be led on by Peter made me angry as did his failure to apologise or take any time explaining the decision he inevitably had to make in order for his family to remain united.

I soldiered on, and a few months later received my own opportunity to move country.

I was approached by the South African hotel chain, *Southern Sun*, with an offer for the position of Front Office Manager on the pre-opening team of their new five-star hotel in Cape Town. This was of great interest to me on two counts; it would provide

*Dangerous Liaisons*

my first department head role as well as experience with a hotel opening, both of which would be beneficial on my resume.

At the time, I was also still struggling with the emotional fall-out from my relationship with Peter and thought that a complete change of environment from London might be good for me. I therefore accepted the offer without fully considering all the implications of such a momentous move.

Since Roberto was my immediate boss, I spoke to him about my proposed resignation to take up a role in South Africa. He tried to talk me out of it, but finally accepted my decision and said I should speak to the General Manager directly before he heard about it from anyone else. I *really* didn't want to have this conversation with RP (as we used to call the GM) since he had a short fuse and was sure he would be angry with me.

As it happened, RP could not have been more understanding. He tried to persuade me to stay, saying that if I wanted a change from London, he could help secure a position in New York or Washington where there were openings in the expanding hotel portfolio of *Four Seasons*.

I knew RP had always been fond of me, even so I was surprised by the level of his support. He told me I had done a great job for the hotel and would be sorely missed if I decided to go. He asked me to give some more thought to my plans, but I assured him my mind was made up. I tendered my letter of resignation to RP, and he replied with a lovely written response which I still treasure all these years later.

On 1 July 1983, almost three years to the day from when I started, I left *Inn on the Park*. RP had been right about the number of opportunities that could have been mine with *Four Seasons*, but I don't think even he could have envisaged the extent to which the company would grow and achieve the global success it enjoys today.

Had I ignored my broken heart and stayed, my career would have panned out way differently. I didn't realise at the time, but this was one of those huge sliding door moments in life and the decision placed me on a very different course from the one I might have imagined just a few months earlier. The career options I was about to discard were hardly a consideration as I was too excited about the new adventure I was about to embark on.

A couple of weeks later, I was booked on a *South African Airways* flight to start a new life in Cape Town.

*There is only one song, with lyrics that say it all, for this conflicted period of my life. It's from the 1981 album by British artist Joan Armatrading, 'Walk Under Ladders'.*

*Playlist Track 9: 'The Weakness In Me'*

# 9

## Cape Town, South Africa

The flight from London took me over the equator into the southern hemisphere and out of summer into the middle of a Cape Town winter. However, it was very different from a British winter. There were many beautiful, mild, sunny days interspersed with some damp dreary weather and on occasions, cold conditions when a southerly wind whipped up from Antarctica over the Cape peninsula.

Cape Town and its surrounds are breathtakingly beautiful. The coastline is dotted with pretty villages built around pristine sandy beaches, while inland are many attractive wineries with their impressive Cape Dutch architecture. The city is overlooked by majestic Table Mountain which I found mesmerising with its constantly changing cloud cover and, under certain conditions, was referred to as having a 'tablecloth' because that is exactly what the clouds looked like cascading over the sides of the flat-topped mountain.

Compared to London, Cape Town is small, even so I found it surprising how little there was to do of an evening until someone told me that the central areas suffered high rates of crime once the offices and shops closed for the day. While it was inadvisable to socialise in the city after dark, there were plenty of beachside suburbs where the atmosphere was more relaxed, and it was to one of those areas that I later moved.

South Africa had been under apartheid rule for many years and by 1983, internal resistance to racial segregation was mounting and becoming increasingly violent. Cape Town was relatively safe compared to Johannesburg, but newcomers to the city like me were given the run-down on the importance of being vigilant in respect to personal security.

I was quite shocked to hear how dangerous the city was, especially coming from London. It quickly became evident that where I formerly lived was much safer than virtually anywhere in South Africa. I began to wish there had been a little more homework conducted on the country I chose to move to.

I realise now how incredibly uninformed I was about the political situation. I would never have lived there had I known the extent of its inequalities which racially segregated every aspect of life from public facilities and social events to housing and employment opportunities.

Since I was white and employed in a luxury hotel, I was sheltered from anything involving the worst of the regime. I also worked with people from many different countries who remained open-minded and fair in their dealings with everyone, regardless of race, so in my little bubble things didn't seem *too* bad. This chapter is not going dwell on the injustices of apartheid as that would be a whole other story, suffice to say it was the main reason I remained in South Africa for only 18 months.

## Cape Town, South Africa

When I arrived, the *Cape Sun* hotel was still in the final stages of construction and fit out, so I was accommodated in one of its sister properties in the city, the *De Waal*. The pre-opening office for *Cape Sun* had also been set up there so I was living and working in the same building.

I was excited to be back in operations and this was my first role as a department head for the front office departments which meant I had quite a large team to supervise. It was also the first opening of my career and, considering how challenging this first experience turned out to be, I'm surprised that I went on to open several more properties later!

The pace of work was manageable initially; developing staffing plans, writing standard operating procedures, setting budgets, organising the lay-out of workspaces and the multitude of other tasks required to get a new hotel up and running. There was also a major game changer coming into play at that time – computers!

In addition to everything else, the management team had to get their heads around a computerised property management system which was a very different beast to the manual systems we had previously worked with.

Not only were we having to learn different processes and set up procedures for a totally new way of operating, but back then computers were far less stable and programmers had limited hotel knowledge. So, between hardware that was frequently breaking down and technicians having to re-write software that functioned the way we the operators needed it to, what can I say? It was exceedingly hard going.

We moved into *Cape Sun* about a month or so before it was due to open, and the situation was becoming ever more chaotic. Construction work was behind schedule and there wasn't a single department which could move into its workspace fully to set everything up as required to commence operations.

This meant that from guest rooms to the kitchens and restaurants, from banqueting suites to the front office and back-of-house areas, progress was hopelessly slow. And this was no small hotel to open. It had 300 rooms, four food and beverage outlets which included French fine dining, an Italian inspired supper/nightclub, Malay style coffee shop and an English tea lounge, plus multiple banqueting areas. The fact that everything was so far behind schedule meant we all knew there would be significant challenges to open in a month's time.

An additional concern was that there were several high-profile international conferences who had booked out the whole property soon after the hotel's opening date. It was no wonder that the General Manager had become a basket case, and several senior managers had either left or been given their marching orders in the later stages of the pre-opening period. But no problem, *Southern Sun* was flying in many of their top managers from around the country to help knock this catastrophe into shape.

Meanwhile, increasing numbers of departmental staff were coming on board to commence their employment and needed to be trained. We were able to cover processes that involved anything manual like the face-to-face check-in process or interactions over the telephone but most of the procedures involved use of the computerised property management system, and that was still a long way from being anywhere near functional.

By this stage, I had found a flat share close to the beach in Sea Point but was mostly living in the hotel since my working day started at around 7.00am and finished after midnight so it was easier to grab a room for a few hours of sleep. There were no days

## Cape Town, South Africa

off and this relentless pace continued for months. One particularly memorable ordeal was working 36 hours straight. No kidding!

Then came the good news... and bad news. The hotel's opening was to be delayed, but only by two weeks so that the large conferences could still be accommodated. This meant we would be opening the hotel at close to full occupancy with no rehearsal time to fine tune or even finalise procedures. Somehow, we pulled it all together and the conference delegates arrived and departed without too many hiccups; however, it required a monumental effort which took its toll on many.

There was a further round of resignations and dismissals after opening which included my immediate boss, the Rooms Division Manager, who was replaced by a long standing and well-respected *Southern Sun* executive.

Bernard was a chain-smoking straight shooter, very different from his gentle predecessor, and had been through a few challenging openings by this stage in his career. He came on board to manage the numerous departments which make up the rooms division of a large property.

Front Office, which I headed up, along with a talented assistant who proved to be a whizz with the computer system, was just about holding its own. But Housekeeping was careering out of control, so that's where Bernard focussed his attention. I had become good friends with the Executive Housekeeper, a lovely Welsh girl called Sam, who had been working at *Southern Sun* for a few years. She had not however managed an opening before and was really struggling to get her department up-and-running effectively.

Bernard could see this immediately and quickly took action to secure a Housekeeper who had been involved with start-ups from one of the company's hotels in Durban. She was another English woman called Susie. Sam was subsequently side-stepped to another five-star property in Cape Town where she was much happier as the hotel had been open for some time and had established systems and procedures in place. I was never as close personally to the new Housekeeper as I was to Sam, but Susie certainly knew her stuff and we worked well together.

The computers eventually settled down to become reasonably stable and my assistant was transferred to the IT division of *Southern Sun* for the roll out of new systems across the group. She was an extremely capable and hard-working young woman who went on to do well in her new role. But that left me without an assistant… Until three, lovely German men showed up, who had just completed an overland adventure from Cairo to Cape Town.

Anton, Carl and Frederick arrived as *Cape Sun* was about to open, and Frederick knew the hotel's General Manager.

He had been advised to stop-by *Cape Sun* when they arrived in town to check out employment opportunities in the new property. All three had previously held hotel management positions in Frankfurt and were quickly offered jobs. Anton became an assistant manager in the coffee shop, while Carl and Frederick joined me in Front Office. I was sceptical of positions being offered because of family connections rather than ability but soon realised that these young men brought with them some top-notch hotel experience and a fine Germanic work ethic. We all hit it off immediately.

The boys moved into a house close to where I was living in Sea Point and one night, Frederick offered me a lift which I gladly accepted after another brutally long working day. I was expecting something relatively modest in terms of vehicle, but he drew up to the main entrance in one of the latest models of a luxury European car.

It transpired that Frederick's father was the senior executive at a prestigious automotive company in Germany, and the car he drove was provided courtesy of the local dealership. Soon after that first lift home, he and I started seeing more of each other socially, together with Anton, Carl and a few other colleagues from the hotel with whom we had become friendly.

Gradually, the workload at *Cape Sun* became more manageable with a regular day off each week allowing for some degree of work-life balance and I began to enjoy a pleasant lifestyle in Cape Town. My German friends loved the outdoors and had plenty of toys to enjoy their active pastimes, including off-road motorbikes, a *Jeep* and speed boat. I was often invited to join them, usually at the behest of Frederick with whom I began a romance. When a beautiful house came up to rent in the fashionable suburb of Fresnaye, which was in the hills overlooking Sea Point with commanding views of the ocean, the decision was made for us all to move in together.

We had so many great times in Cape Town. When not out on the boat exploring remote beaches and enjoying a barbeque, we would be in the outback, off-roading on a powerful motorbike.

Frederick was very capable of handling himself around anything motorised but his fearlessness and need for speed left me quite petrified at times. He was most generous, and I received some beautiful gifts as well as being taking to the finest restaurants in and around Cape Town. On one occasion, Frederick asked me to join him on a friend's private plane to visit Germany for a family celebration he was attending, which I declined due to work commitments – truly!

It sure was a long way from life in the small town where I grew up. I would speak to Mum on the phone to keep her updated of my news, and she was always so happy to hear that I was having a good life, but at the same time missed not seeing me. I assured her that I probably wouldn't stay in South Africa for long and may be home in the not-too-distant future.

Mum and I also used to write letters to each other, as international telephone calls were expensive in those days, and I knew what an effort this would have been on her part as she hadn't received much of an education. I cherished every one of those letters Mum sent, and it still makes me emotional when I think about the time and love she put into them.

After living in South Africa for over a year, the four of us sharing the house in Fresnaye began talking more seriously about returning to Europe. We loved Cape Town on many levels; however, the apartheid regime was intolerable and offensive to us. Carl particularly struggled as he was in a serious relationship with a Cape Malay girl. Since we lived in a 'white only' area, all of us would have been in serious trouble had the authorities discovered that his girlfriend stayed over at our house several nights every week.

Each of us made plans for our departure and resigned our positions at the hotel. The mass resignation was not well received but there was no doubt we'd all paid our dues to ensure the opening success of *Cape Sun*. I've had some hard gigs in hospitality, but none was tougher than this first role as a department head leading a team through a very challenging opening.

The whole experience was the nail in the coffin for Frederick as far as a career in hotel management was concerned. He could not believe how demanding the work was for the relative pittance of a salary. He planned to hot foot it back to Frankfurt and have a serious conversation about joining his father's

## Cape Town, South Africa

company. And that he did. We continued our relationship after Cape Town, but the challenges of living in different countries became increasingly difficult.

After leaving *Cape Sun*, we wanted to enjoy a holiday and see more of the country so took off in the *Jeep* for a few weeks. It was a wonderful trip travelling all the way up to the Mozambique border, staying at luxury hotels along the way in some beautiful coastal and game park locations. A grand finale to our life in South Africa.

I arrived at Gatwick Airport on a bitterly cold winters day in February 1985, but Mum and Dad's joyous faces and warm welcome more than made up for the weather. After the lifestyle I had enjoyed in Cape Town, it was surreal to be back in our small family home. At the same time though, I enjoyed having mother fuss over me. My plan was to head back to London as soon as I could and, after a couple of weeks, I returned to my studio apartment in Wimbledon.

What next, I wondered? I did not imagine that within six months another opportunity would be tempting me overseas again. But to somewhere very different and not quite so far away as Cape Town.

*We threw many parties at the house in Fresnaye and one of our favourite albums was Lionel Richie's chart topper, 'Can't Slow Down', which came out in 1983. I've selected one of its big singles which always takes me back to those Cape Town days.*

*Playlist Track 10: 'Running With The Night'*

# 10

# An Idyllic Greek Island

---

On returning to London, I began the search for a suitable position to further my career.

The role I accepted led to taking my first steps into the world of boutique hotels – though in 1985, small, individualised properties were not referred to as 'boutique' they were just regarded as rather quirky. The hotel was *Dukes* in St James, with 52 rooms and located in one of the pretty side streets behind Green Park, where I was offered employment as House Manager which involved overseeing the rooms division departments of the property.

*Dukes* is a delightful hotel steeped in history and quintessential English charm. Its legendary bar, famous for the quality of martinis served, is said to be the inspiration for James Bond's classic line, *'Shaken not stirred.'*

I was once again making the long commute from Wimbledon on public transport which was tiresome after having grown accustomed to a 15-minute drive in Cape Town. The return to British weather was also quite a shock to the system after the climate in South Africa. I tried my best to ignore these downsides because I was happy to be back in the buzz of London and enjoying a busy social life with old friends.

Then, unexpectedly, another of life's sliding door moments presented when *Dukes'* Executive Housekeeper resigned, and I advertised for a replacement. There was a weekly publication in those days of a magazine *'The Caterer and Hotelkeeper'* which virtually everyone in the industry subscribed to and was the go-to place for posting vacancies of any relatively senior position for most hospitality organisations.

I wasn't looking for another job in the 'Positions Vacant' section, but adjacent to the role I posted for a Housekeeper was another which caught my attention. I quickly read it and put the magazine away. Half an hour later, I took another look to check out the advertisement properly. The job was listed as: *'Overseas Property Manager in Greek Islands for Upmarket Tour Operator.'*

I closed my office door and picked up the telephone.

The following week, I was interviewed by the Managing Director of *Greek Island Destinations (GID)* at his office in Surrey. The company had been operating packaged holidays (flights, accommodation and transfers) for several years to some of the more remote and less commercialised islands in Greece.

Adam explained to me that their management couple on Paxos, Charles and Alice, were retiring at the end of the current season and he was in the process of recruiting a new manager to take over from them. Paxos, a small island in the Ionian, had been the company's initial foray into the holiday market where they now managed around 30 properties consisting of villas, cottages and apartments which were rented to tourists for their summer vacation.

In addition to accommodation, there was a sailing and windsurfing centre as well as a fleet of motorised dinghies which could be hired for all or part of the visitor's holiday, as some of the best beaches were only accessible by boat.

*GID* also operated on other islands in the Ionian – Cephalonia, Zakynthos, Ithaca and Kythira – which they had expanded to over the years after the early days of building a successful family business on Paxos.

It had all begun back in the 1970s when the business founders discovered a picturesque island south of Corfu. The couple fell in love with the place and built a house on a beautiful stretch of coastline where long summer holidays were enjoyed with their family.

They introduced friends to Paxos who were equally enchanted by the beauty, simplicity and remoteness of the island. Before long, an idea was hatched to lease properties from local owners for the summer, combine this accommodation with flights and transfers, then sell to overseas clients, mostly from Britain. From the outset, the offering was marketed as exclusive and certainly not your run-of-the-mill 'package holiday'.

The couple succeeded with their ambitious plans, and by 1985 had a thriving business operating on five beautiful Greek islands. Paxos, however, remained the closest to their hearts for obvious reasons.

Adam, who I liked from the outset, was the couple's eldest son and had been Managing Director of *GID* for several years. He shared with me his wealth of knowledge about the business, its history and future direction – as well as the pitfalls to be aware of when working in a small island community.

It all sounded pretty good to me, even though this role represented something of a side-step from a more typical career in hotel management. My father was horrified when I informed him that I was seriously considering making another move and told me I needed to knuckle down and stop 'flitting around'. And I retaliated by saying the world was changing, and young people were not prepared to stay in one job for life, unlike his generation.

In due course, the role with *GID* was offered to me and soon after plans were taking shape to uproot my life again.

Adam wanted to introduce me to the team in Greece as well as provide a basic orientation, so he and I travelled together from London to Paxos. It was early August at the height of the European summer and holiday season which meant the island's staff were feeling the heat and hectic pace of work, but to me it all looked idyllic. I was charmed by Paxos from the moment I arrived.

Adam was only able to remain with me for a short time before returning to the UK office and, when he departed, I was left under the guidance of local managers, Charles and Alice. At that point, my status became significantly diminished. It was made clear to me by them that I was not working in a management capacity and would be treated like anyone else on the team. Hmmm…

One of the first issues to arise was the accommodation arrangements. When I was offered the position, it included my own apartment in which to live. On the way over to Paxos,

Adam had broken the news that since they were fully booked during August, would I mind sharing an apartment with another member of staff for a short time. I didn't object to this as I figured there wasn't much choice in the matter anyway.

After a few weeks, when I knew there was a property available, Charles declined my request to move saying that it would set a precedent for others on the team to ask for their own accommodation and anyway, *'It's late in the season, therefore hardly worth all the effort.'*

But hang on, I thought, I was recruited as a manager with an apartment as part of the deal. Never mind, I had become friendly with the girl in my flat share, so I tolerated the situation. Nonetheless, as someone who values their privacy, it was a big deal for me at the time.

The managers were constantly reminding me that I *'had a lot to learn'* and my prior work experiences counted for little on Paxos. This situation where my abilities were being questioned and undermined was a first for me.

Although I was dissatisfied with some aspects of the work environment, I was loving the lifestyle of living on a beautiful Greek island. So, I decided that if I was going to be treated like any other staff member, I would start to act like one by socialising and participating in all the after-hours fun.

By the end of the season, Charles and Alice had determined that I was not suitable to step into their shoes. I briefed Adam on my disappointment about the way I'd been treated after he left Paxos, and he was sympathetic. However, he also felt that managing the island's operations was too great of a responsibility for one person. It had therefore been decided for the following season that I would be working alongside an older manager as their assistant. The person recruited was a retired Army officer who, it was probably felt, would be able to keep the 'rank-and-file' in order as effectively as Charles.

Despite this rather wobbly start to my tenure with *GID*, I could see potential for future progression and decided to stay on. After completing close down procedures on Paxos at the end of the summer, I returned to Britain and worked in the company's office.

During that winter I holidayed in Florida with Frederick, as by then he was working in America. I realised during this reunion, some six months after we'd last caught up in London, that my feelings were probably not sufficiently strong to maintain a long-term distance relationship and resigned myself to the fact that, with him residing in California and me on a remote Greek island, things would eventually fizzle out. And within another few months, they had.

Before heading to Paxos for my second season, *GID* enrolled me to attend Greek language school in Athens. I endured four weeks of immersive classes which I found challenging. It was important though if I was to pursue a career with the company that I had at least some basic knowledge of the language, given that most of the locals on Paxos didn't speak English. The Europeans in class who already spoke several languages took to the intricacies of Greek like ducks to water, but I was far less proficient. This surprised me as French was one of my best subjects at school, so had assumed I might be linguistically gifted. I am not!

From Athens, I flew to Corfu and then travelled to Paxos on the public ferry. The *Kamelia* was a decrepit rust bucket of a boat, God knows how old, but it was the only means of transport to and from the island at that time. Its decaying condition was the reason *GID* privately chartered a modern vessel for their clients during the summer. I shared the three-hour journey with many of the locals who had been to Corfu for shopping, doctor appointments and other goods and services they required which were not available on Paxos.

Accompanying passengers to the island was an array of wildlife, so there was much clucking, baa-ing and barking on board – especially during the heavy swell in the section of transfer which is on open sea!

I was met in Paxos by Charles and Alice who had arrived a few days earlier with the new Island Manager whom they were inducting into their previous role. George was in his late 50s and not at all overbearing given his background, in fact quite a gentle man.

Throughout March, key members of the overseas team arrived to commence the pre-opening work for the new season. PK, the long-serving Boats Manager, was the first to arrive, then Ben the new Chief Sailing Instructor and soon after came Ed, who didn't have a title, possibly because he was such an oddball.

Ed had been looking after the *GID* properties on Paxos for a few years and so his contrariness was tolerated because he knew the tricks to fixing up a few of the more rundown properties and making them habitable for the summer. The rest of the staff arrived in April a few of weeks ahead of the first holiday bookings for the season.

Charles and Alice departed and left Paxos in the hands of a new management team for the first time since they had first joined the company around eight years earlier. George was now in charge with me as his assistant manager.

As might be imagined, there are many minor and major incidents to be handled when you're dealing with clients and staff on a 24/7 basis, the management of which can be challenging at the best of times, even in a city.

In a remote and relatively undeveloped location such as Paxos with few facilities – no airport, no hospital, limited food and extremely limited water supplies – those challenges can escalate to another level. Sometimes there can be an unusual run of trying situations and, as it turned out, my second term on Paxos certainly did not lack drama. In fact, it turned into a real doozy of a season…as well as being when I met my future husband.

The first of several unfortunate incidents to befall us took place early in the pre-opening period when the Sailing Centre Manager needed to pick up supplies from Corfu. Panni, an agent who handled some of the local business affairs for *GID*, advised Ben to take the public ferry due to adverse weather conditions. Instead, Ben decided to sail over alone in the company yacht.

Predictably, he encountered difficulties, ran aground off Corfu and had to be rescued by coastguards. Ben was fortunate to sustain only minor injuries, but the yacht required significant and expensive repair work. Panni had to attend Corfu and calm the situation with authorities, which he was none too happy about since Ben had ignored his advice about taking the yacht over in the first place.

Shortly afterwards, we were having our regular morning team meeting at the office when one of the sailing instructors staggered in with blood pouring down his face and in an obvious state of shock.

He'd crashed the company pick-up truck while driving from the sailing centre which was located at the other end of the island. We cleaned him up and luckily his injuries were not severe, even so he needed to be checked out properly and was put on a sea taxi over to the *Corfu Private Clinic*. All the *GID* staff were covered by company medical insurance and treatment at the private facility in Corfu, as the public hospital there was too basic.

The reasonably serious incidents noted above are in addition to the regular day to day unpredictability of managing a tourism business in an isolated location.

Clients invariably present their own set of challenges when unhappy with any aspect of their holiday, which sometimes may be completely out of the operator's control – like the weather, for example – and the manager must work around their complaints to find an amicable solution.

The young staff who were out partying most nights and sometimes didn't show up for work the next day were another source of angst for the unfortunate manager to deal with. Then there was the in-fighting between individuals who didn't get on with each other – it's not easy when everyone is living and working together on a small island.

Handling the locals could also lead to some stressful encounters. There were instances of the owner of a property secretly moving back into their house if it wasn't booked by tourists for an odd week or two during the season, even though *GID* had paid them and expected vacant possession for the whole summer. Sometimes, clients had to be moved at short notice to another property which was believed to be vacant, only to find that the Greek owners were back in residence there!

Therefore, it was no surprise to me when, just a few weeks into the season, George concluded that the Paxos gig was not for him and left to pursue a more relaxed lifestyle back in England.

I wondered whether Charles and Alice would be recalled but it was decided that Jack, the youngest son of *GID's* owner, would transfer from one of the other islands and take up the role of manager on Paxos.

Jack was a similar age to me, and we got along quite well together. He was familiar with Paxos from spending family holidays there and subsequent visits after he joined the business, plus he had an excellent command of the Greek language which was very useful. He was aware of the early season turmoil and set about providing greater stability to move forward for a successful summer.

One of new recruits for 1986 was a lovely young man called Ken who had joined *GID* to work on the boating operations with PK. He was from London and had previously been employed on the oil rigs in the freezing North Sea, so was delighted to find himself in the far more agreeable environment of Paxos.

Ken was good looking and friendly with an excellent work ethic. He also had a wicked sense of humour which made him popular from the get-go. Ken wasn't (and still isn't) a 'blokey' kind of guy and seemed to prefer hanging out with the girls when socialising. He would have regular dinners and catch ups with the office reps who were all female, and I was usually included.

A couple of months into the season, Ken and I became romantically involved. We realised this would probably not go down too well due to our respective positions and also because I was a fair bit older – Ken was 20 and I was 29 when we met – so tried to keep our relationship under wraps. This was unlikely to last given the environment in which we lived and worked.

The season progressed and staff settled into their routine of the morning meeting followed by visiting clients, administrative duties, handling maintenance issues, checking housekeeping standards and myriad other tasks.

In common with most other businesses on the island, our office closed at lunchtime for afternoon siesta which allowed everyone to rest or go to the beach during the hottest part of the day, before returning to work for a couple of hours in the evening.

At the end of the working day, it was time for a few beers and a spot of people-watching in the main square while considering where to have dinner that night. We would alternate the tavernas frequented so that locals wouldn't be offended by us favouring some over others, although of course we had our favourites.

One was an Italian pizzeria which offered a welcome change of menu from variations of grilled fish, souvlaki and Greek salad which were the mainstay of the majority of the island's restaurants. Sometimes, a group of us would get together and cook at home utilising whatever we could muster from the limited range of food available in the shops. Beer and wine were always in plentiful supply, however.

After dinner, we would often head off to one of the bars. And we did have a definite favourite when it came to a late-night watering hole – *The Carnayo*.

The bar was run by two enterprising locals who had other tourism-related businesses on Paxos which kept them extremely busy throughout the summer to a point where they hardly slept. Like many others who lived on the island, they would catch up on their rest during the winter when the island closed to tourists.

The work with *GID* could be demanding at times but the overall lifestyle was amazing, and I can't think of anyone (other than perhaps George) who didn't look back to their days on Paxos with great fondness.

A month or so into our relationship when it was becoming obvious that there was something going on, Ken and I decided we should open up about our involvement. As is often the case, after the initial 'scandal' broke with its accompanying gossip, everyone moved on quite quickly. Even Jack, who was none too impressed initially, soon got over it particularly when a couple of more serious incidents occurred which demanded his (and my) attention. The summer of '86 finished as it had begun – with a fair bit of drama.

In the town square one evening during August, I was approached by a local informing me about an accident involving Ken.

A few minutes later, a truck pulled into town with Ken unconscious in the back together with a puppy we had rescued earlier in the year. He had been driving his moped to a remote property on the island with the puppy snuggled in his backpack when he met another motorbike coming around a tight bend on the wrong side of the road causing a collision.

Ken was launched over the handlebars of his vehicle, hit the ground forcefully and suffered a concussion in the process. The dear little dog, who was uninjured, was quietly whimpering by Ken's side on the road when a truck driver stopped to help. The tourist responsible for the accident was unhurt.

The only doctor on the island was still on duty in his surgery and, after a quick examination, advised that a transfer to the *Corfu Private Clinic* was required immediately. A high-speed water taxi and driver were quickly rustled up. It was by now

## An Idyllic Greek Island

about 8.30pm which meant the three-hour crossing would be in darkness.

There was no question that I would accompany Ken, and I had a friend on holiday in Paxos at the time who insisted on coming too, which I really appreciated. Ken was loaded in to the small boat on a stretcher with a drip in his arm, which was a mixture of pain killers and a sedative. It was a harrowing trip, but the driver did a commendable job of getting us to Corfu as safely, smoothly and quickly as possible.

The Paxos doctor had called ahead, and an ambulance awaited us on arrival at the harbour to take Ken straight into emergency for tests. It was past midnight by this time.

Eventually, Ken reappeared heavily sedated and was placed in a comfortable private room. I was advised that he had several injuries which were fairly superficial, but the major concern was a fractured cheek bone. The medical advice was for Ken to remain flat on his back in bed, move as little as possible and that the bone would repair itself in a week or so. It didn't sound very convincing to me. As the days rolled by, Ken continued to be in a great deal of pain with the swelling on his face around the injury becoming progressively worse.

I spoke to Jack a few times, who shared my concerns, and it was determined to have Ken fly back to the UK as soon as he could manage the journey. On arrival to hospital in London, he was admitted for surgery straight away after being told that the cheek was quite badly injured and should have been operated on within 24 hours to avoid further complications. Because it had been so long since the accident, Ken's injury had started to mend, but incorrectly, so the London surgeon had to re-break the bone in order to fix it properly. Ouch!

After a couple of weeks convalescing at home, Ken returned to Paxos for the last month of the season by which stage he had become quite the local hero. Everyone was glad to see he had made a full recovery after a rather nasty accident.

And the final drama of the summer? Well, that involved a house, which was leased for the season by *GID*, burning down. One of the staff had been testing a rat catching device he designed and built to which there was an electrical element that had apparently 'shorted' and ignited the timber roof of the property.

The staff member was staying there overnight to monitor the device which was fortunate in that he was able to raise the alarm quickly and luckily was not harmed himself. The house was a shell after the fire and the owner was understandably none too impressed. I'm sure *GID* had a lot of explaining to do. I would also imagine that the company's insurance premiums increased dramatically after the 1986 season!

We completed closing procedures in October and left the island to return for the winter break in England. It was confirmed that I would return to Paxos the following year as Manager (finally) and Ken was appointed as the new Boats Manager.

In November, I attended the International Tour Operators Association (ITOA) conference for *GID* being held on the Gold Coast, Australia. This trip introduced me to Australia and was instrumental in influencing a later decision to migrate there.

After Christmas, I returned to Athens for intermediate Greek classes which were even more punishing than the previous year's beginner classes!

Afterwards, I travelled the by now familiar route to Paxos via Corfu, meeting up with Ken along the way. Spring in Paxos is quite lovely with the island slowly coming back to life after a cold, wet winter. There would be only one taverna open where many of the local men (and the odd woman) hung out, and you may never see some of them again until the end of the season when all the tourists had left. The pre and post season weeks gave one a true taste of the island's culture and its isolation, which I always really enjoyed.

We knew it was going to be an unusually busy season, the reason being that Paxos had been featured in Britain's leading holiday programme on the *BBC* during the winter. This had been filmed on the island, amongst all the other drama, during the previous summer.

*GID* featured strongly in the Paxos segment and the response from viewers was immediate. The season was extended by several weeks to accommodate the additional demand for bookings. Capacity occupancy of properties, boats and sailing holidays usually only occurred during the month of August. In 1987, however, bookings for all areas of the operation were choc-o-bloc from June to the end of September. Other operators on the island were experiencing similar levels of demand so obviously this was going to be a very big year. It was indeed a record-breaking season for *GID*.

Anyone who has worked in hospitality knows how stressful it is to maintain peak business for long periods of time. For example, if there is a serious maintenance problem in a property but alternate accommodation is available you can simply move the client and this generally keeps everyone satisfied. Should you be fully booked though, the problem must be managed as best you can.

On the water, our dinghies and sailing craft were under pressure for much longer than usual. While there were back-up engines and hulls for the boating operation and spares of all the 'stuff' that makes things sail, we underestimated just how many replacements were required for such a bumper period of trade so were constantly trying to improvise with whatever we had available until parts arrived from the UK. Sometimes, there was more equipment than clients being loaded on to our flights from London!

And how did the newly appointed Island Manager fare in this hectic environment where there was little back-up if something went wrong? I think I did okay but only thanks to an incredible team effort. We had our usual ups-and-downs, but no-one had time to dwell on petty issues.

Adam and Jack took turns to support me on Paxos whenever either could manage a week or two on the island. I really appreciated this as I knew both had commitments in other areas of the business which also required their time and attention. But the biggest debt of gratitude was to Ken for his enormous contribution throughout that summer. He willingly took on many of the tasks I couldn't get to, even though they were seldom part of his job description. I really do think that I might have sunk without him there personally committed to my welfare. Thankfully, we didn't have any of the major incidents with which we'd had to contend the previous year. But still...

There were ferocious heatwave conditions for several weeks when daytime temperatures ran to the mid-40s and overnight, remained close to 30 degrees Celsius. Air conditioners were few and far between on Paxos, so it just had to be sweated out. Everyone lost weight that summer!

Ken also had his challenges dealing with a heavy drinking off-sider who, we learnt as the season progressed, was opening his first cans of beer at around 10am each day and didn't stop drinking until *The Carnayo* kicked him out in the early hours of the following morning.

Additionally, there was a disappearing act from our maintenance man Richard, Ed's assistant for the season. Richard was quite a character – charming, well-spoken and certainly not your typical mister fix-it.

One day, he jumped on the *Kamelia* for a supposed day trip to Corfu and never returned. No-one heard another word from him. Much speculation surrounded our dear Richard who I'd thought from the outset to be a rather mysterious individual… Or maybe he just didn't like the job on Paxos… Or working with Ed?!

By the end of the season, discussions began again about roles for the following year and who was intending to stay on with the company. Any initial misgivings about my suitability for a management role were dispelled by the end of 1987, but I wasn't sure about returning, wondering whether it was time to focus on greater career progression.

With that in mind, Adam and I talked about a regional role for me to oversee the operations on several islands. But after some consideration, I decided that the gypsy life of an island roving position was not something that appealed to me. It would also have created challenges in my relationship with Ken. I had by then turned 30 and felt I should be thinking about settling down into a long-term personal commitment. Ken and I made the decision that it was time to move on from *GID* and pursue other opportunities together.

What we were going to do and where to next, were the questions which would dominate the next few months.

Before moving on, a word about the two puppies Ken and I rescued from a garbage bin in the early days of our first season on Paxos. They were both female and looked like labradors so were most endearing.

As the end of summer approached, we were becoming increasingly concerned about their care when we left the island over winter. The Paxos bus driver let us know he was interested in taking the two of them back to his property on the mainland and train them as gun dogs.

The local agent Panni assured us that the puppies were going to a good home; however, we knew it would be a very different life for them. It was agreed that if the girls didn't settle, they would be returned to us in Paxos the following season. We didn't see them again and the updates received were always positive which put our minds (somewhat) at ease.

The following year, we adopted another discarded puppy who we found on the roadside. We raised this little fellow and called him 'Noy-Noy', after the Greek brand of evaporated milk we fed him on to build up his strength, and which he loved.

Noy-Noy wound up having an enviable life travelling all over the island on boats, cars and motorbikes with Ken and me. I was much happier with the rehoming arrangements for him at the end of the season. A lovely Italian lady, Katie, who had been operating a business on Paxos for many years, came forward with an offer to take Noy-Noy as she thought he would be great company for her other dog. She subsequently took both pets back and forth between Italy for the winter and Greece each summer.

When I saw Noy-Noy a few years later while on holiday in Paxos, he looked healthy and well loved. However, Katie shared with me a story that broke my heart. Apparently, after I had farewelled Noy-Noy and handed him over to her at the harbour when I left the island, he would thereafter take off each evening and run down to meet the ferry returning from Corfu, patiently watching and waiting, no doubt hoping I would step off the boat. Only after the last passenger had disembarked would he, rather dejectedly, return home to Katie. She told me that Noy-Noy did this *every day* for six months. Ahhh...

And so, to the music which takes me back to those years I spent in the mid-80s on an enchanting Greek island. It was hard to select just one or two songs for this chapter, but I settled on the following.

The Carnayo Bar, where we spent so many late nights, constantly played what became one of the biggest albums of all time. 'Brothers In Arms' was released in 1985 by Dire Straits, and I've selected its opening track.

Playlist Track 11: 'So Far Away'

The second is a lively number which was guaranteed to get everyone on the dance floor at the Paxos disco. This outdoor venue was only open for a few weeks in the middle of summer and all the GID team would be there along with young locals and tourists, dancing the night away under the stars. The song is from 1987 and one of Whitney Houston's most successful singles.

Playlist Track 12: 'I Wanna Dance with Somebody (Who Loves Me)'

## 11

## Shattered Dreams

After returning from Greece, Ken and I spent time evaluating our options for the future. We were not keen to remain in London and thought that exploring a new country might be fun. It was decided that job prospects for both of us would be better in an English-speaking country. We then seriously began investigating possibilities of a move to Canada or Australia, due to the relative ease of entry and work permits for British citizens in either of those countries.

Canada was preferred because of its relative proximity to the UK, but ultimately, Australia was our choice because of its more favourable climate, even though it was on the other side of the world.

Ken was still young enough to obtain a 12-month working holiday visa for Australia which was a quick and straight forward process. However, at 30 I was too old and had to make a much lengthier application for permanent residency.

I applied on the 'points' system which was based on age, level of education and previous work experience. I had the required 70 points for entry and my timing was fortunate as, just a few years later, the eligibility level was raised, meaning I would not have qualified.

The granting of my permanent residency proved to be fortuitous as it provided options to stay in Australia long term. Our plan was that should we decide to remain in the country for longer than 12 months, we would make an application for Ken to become a resident on de facto grounds with me, which in fact is what eventuated.

After emotional farewells to both sets of parents at Heathrow Airport, we were on our way for an Australian adventure. It was exciting but, with no idea of where in that vast land we planned to settle and no jobs lined up, also somewhat daunting.

We arrived in Sydney which surprisingly didn't appeal to us. This was probably because we stayed in a rather seedy bed-and-breakfast in Kings Cross surrounded by junkies, sex workers and the homeless. *The Cross* was very rough in 1988, and we wanted to get out of there as quickly as possible.

It's a pity we didn't spend more time to check out other areas as we would doubtless have found an attractive location in which to pursue the possibilities of a future life in Sydney.

Instead, we flipped a coin to decide whether we should move on to either Perth or Far North Queensland. I can't remember why we limited ourselves to those two locations, but the coin flip determined that Queensland was to be the go, which was lucky, as I don't think either of us had fully considered the remoteness of Western Australia.

## Shattered Dreams

The next few months were not easy as we journeyed south down the coast of Queensland from town to town and found nowhere particularly appealing. Our funds were also dwindling which added further anxiety to our situation. We purchased a vehicle which was a cost-effective means of travelling in a state the size of Queensland and a place to sleep if we became really desperate.

I was in touch with a recruitment agent in Sydney who lined up an interview for the position of Reception Manager on *Hayman Island*. I was offered the role but declined the opportunity since both Ken and I figured we'd had enough of island life for a while. We thought nearby Airlie Beach on the mainland might be a place to consider and found casual work in the town. After about three months though we decided this wasn't where we wanted to settle longer term.

I can safely say that by then we were *not* having a love affair with this land down under! We discussed the Gold Coast as a possibility, based on my knowledge of the area from when I attended a conference there for *Greek Island Destinations*, and decided to visit the region and check it out properly. We determined that this was going to be a last-ditch effort to find somewhere that felt right for us, otherwise we would pack up and return to London.

The Gold Coast appealed immediately. The ocean and beaches were breathtaking, and the weather far more congenial than the intense heat and humidity of further north. An additional bonus was that suitable job opportunities existed for both of us. And that was where we settled in Australia. Ken still lives there today.

We rented an awful apartment, but there was little choice since accommodation was in short supply and expensive. The area was enjoying a tourist boom due to Australia's bi-centennial celebrations, as well as Brisbane hosting a World Expo.

After a few months when the peak of those events had passed, we were able to move into another a much nicer property for the same rent as we had been paying at 'cockie kingdom' (which was how we referred to the first cockroach infested flat!).

Ken found work with a communications company. Initially, he installed car telephones but later moved into a sales role which coincided with the advent of mobile phones. Ken was a gifted salesman, not the smooth-talking type, but someone who really listened to what a customer needed and then recommended whatever was most suitable and cost-effective for them. He thoroughly researched his company's products, as well as those of competitors, and his detailed knowledge of the communications market won him many loyal customers.

I accepted the role of Front Office Manager (FOM) at a newly opened resort. Since I was the third FOM to have been appointed in a short space of time it seemed likely there would be some challenges in store for me. And that turned out to be correct.

The hotel had opened with high occupancies due to demand created by the bi-centennial and World Expo events. From previous experience, I knew how punishing this would have been for a new team and by the time I arrived the large property felt more than a little chaotic.

Once again, I found myself with computer issues to contend with and a system that was constantly failing. I cannot begin to calculate the number of hours I worked, sometimes all through the night, running makeshift manual procedures to keep the operation functioning whilst the computer support team tried to resuscitate the property management system. It was a total nightmare.

The front-line staff had been recruited for their looks and personality, rather than any previous hotel exposure. This can work so long as a comprehensive training programme exists which is rolled out effectively. Unfortunately, formal pre-opening training appeared to have been sketchy, so everyone was just doing their own thing.

Where to start? There are many things I am *not* good at, however, the ability to establish priorities in a particular situation is one of my strengths.

The most serious issue was with the large number of invoices for groups who had previously stayed at the hotel, as these all had significant balances outstanding and remained unpaid since the companies to whom they were issued had numerous queries and could not reconcile the amounts with their own records. I began re-constructing scores of accounts to align with the reservation documentation and, though it took several months, I managed to obtain settlement for all the invoices which had remained unpaid since those early days of the hotel opening. I was a big hit with the Financial Controller!

Gradually, I was able to start working on other priorities and within a few weeks, there was some light emerging from the chaos. The team could sense they had a manager who was going to stick around and fix the problems and began to take a more responsible attitude to their work. It helped that the hotel was by then less busy, and we had time to conduct some proper training.

The General Manager, a very capable but demanding European, also realised he had at last found a reasonably competent FOM. Johan Wagner was not the easiest person to work for but he was a manager I came to hold in high regard. I learned a lot from him. Johan was incredibly driven and instrumental in guiding the new resort to become a highly successful business.

The demands of my new position were being received none too well at home. Ken had not previously experienced me working in hotel management and the time commitment it required. Understandably, he grew increasingly frustrated at the number of hours I spent at work. I loved my job though and admit I often put its needs ahead of my partner's. We generally got along well together but the dedication to my job continued to be the cause of many disagreements throughout the course of our relationship.

Ken and I made new friends in our respective workplaces, and we began to have an active social life on the Gold Coast. Both of us were on good salaries which meant our financial position was much improved and I thought we had settled into our new life quite well, hence was surprised when Ken brought up the subject of returning to the UK. He was much closer to his parents than I and confided how much he missed and worried about them. He wasn't discounting a return to Australia in future but needed to check on his family before committing to a country on the other side of the world.

I realised that Ken was serious about going back and had obviously been thinking about it for some time so agreed to his proposal. We had to fast track his application for permanent residency so that a potential return to Australia would be straight forward. Before we left, Ken was successfully granted permanent residency on de facto grounds with me.

We awoke to a cold, foggy November morning on our first day in Britain. Ken and I looked at each other and agreed that after the excitement of returning home, we were faced with a reality check. Nevertheless, we determined to make a go of things in the UK for as long as possible.

We both found excellent jobs quite quickly – Ken, once again, in sales with a communications company in London while I was recruited for an opening as Rooms Division Manager at a beautiful country house hotel. *Hanbury Manor*, located just outside London in Hertfordshire, was a renovated and extended mansion on 200 acres of grounds which incorporated a championship golf course designed by Jack Nicklaus. Ken and I lived on site in a charming cottage that had been built as part of the original estate in the late 19th century.

*Hanbury Manor* was another challenging opening but, by then, I had a good deal more familiarity with start-ups. A very capable group of people were employed and together we quickly formed a close-knit team. The original manor had been extended to house 98 guest rooms, two restaurants overseen by award winning chef Albert Roux, several banqueting rooms which included a deconsecrated church, a stunning indoor pool, day spa and country club. There were also several luxury residential properties built around the golf course which were sold off to private individuals.

It was a terrific property, and my time there remains one of the highlights of my career.

The positions that Ken and I now worked in represented significant advancement in terms of salary and conditions of employment, which we were both thrilled about. Ken had a smart new company car and was commuting to North London each day which he didn't find too onerous. I merely had to step out of our cottage and cross the hotel's ornate walled garden to my office.

The days and months moved along pleasantly. The possibility of returning to Australia was discussed many times and we eventually decided that was where we wanted to be. Since there was a time limit for re-entry on our visas, Ken and I started making plans to head down under once again.

In November 1991, we had flights booked for the return journey. Shortly before our departure, I received a call from my old boss on the Gold Coast who had no idea I was about to arrive back there. Johan telephoned me on the off chance that I might consider a return to my previous position at the resort.

I jumped at the offer since Australia was struggling through an economic recession at that time and friends had warned us that jobs were few and far between. I don't think Johan could believe his luck, and neither could I!

I would go on to stay at the resort for over three years and be promoted to Deputy General Manager along the way. When Ken arrived on the Gold Coast, his previous employer also offered him a job back with the company, in a senior sales role. We counted ourselves very fortunate to have been given these opportunities when unemployment rates in the country were generally high.

Arriving in Australia the second time around, Ken and I felt a much greater sense of belonging than during our first period in the country. This I think would never have been the case had we *not* returned to London. The 'what if we went back' scenario had been laid to rest. We easily picked up where we left off with jobs and friends from our previous time on the Gold Coast.

After renting for about a year, we were excited to move into the new house we'd built. It was the home of our dreams compared to what we could have afforded in London. As soon as the property was securely fenced, we bought two beautiful golden retriever puppies, which for me was another dream come true. Jake and Benson, who were siblings from the same litter, quickly became a cherished part of our family. Life was good.

While we had been in London, Ken had broached the subject with his parents about the possibility of them migrating to

Australia after we returned there. As soon as we were living in our new house, a holiday was arranged for John and Margaret to help them decide for themselves about a potential permanent move. Unsurprisingly, they were most enthusiastic to progress their migration plans after their vacation on the Gold Coast.

We perhaps should have been a little more cautious, knowing that a holiday compared to the reality of day-to-day life can be a very different proposition. But hey, who wants to dampen the excitement of it all? And so, we forged ahead with making all the necessary arrangements and were able to secure resident visas for John and Margaret based on 'family reunion' with their son.

I remember Ken saying shortly before his parents were due to arrive that he was content with our life as it was, and expressed concerns about how things might change. I didn't share his worries at all (but perhaps should have) as I was fond of John and Margaret and knew how much happier Ken would be to have his parents close by, instead of constantly worrying about them living on a council estate in London.

Ken thought his parents needed a job and a 'purpose' as soon as they arrived in Australia. I disagreed, wanting them to first find their feet and then decide how they wished to spend their time. Ken was convinced they could run a little café since both were talented cooks. I was flabbergasted to put it mildly. But Ken went ahead anyway and took out a lease on a small shop not far from where we lived.

I'll not detail the events that followed, only that after Ken's parents came to Australia, our lives did indeed change dramatically. However, perhaps John and Margaret's move was merely the catalyst for change. Issues between Ken and I had already become apparent before his parents arrived and we were increasingly at odds with each other on the direction of our lives. Regardless, we resolved to work through our differences.

A year-or-so later, Ken was offered an opportunity in corporate sales for *Telstra* based in Brisbane. It presented as not only a good career move for him but also provided some physical distance from his parents on the Gold Coast which we thought might be beneficial. Our 'dream home' was sold and we bought a charming *Queenslander* to renovate in the Brisbane suburb of Paddington.

By then, I had left my position at the resort and was helping John and Margaret run their café. I decided after moving to Brisbane it was time to get back into a 'proper' job, but not hospitality.

I felt like a change and thought to try my hand in real estate sales. I did in fact really enjoy the work and was quite successful in selling residential properties in the inner-city suburbs surrounding Paddington.

In the meantime, John and Margaret struggled to manage their café alone and the move to *Telstra* for Ken was not really working out for him either. It's hardly surprising that with so much negativity in our lives, the relationship between Ken and I was going from bad to worse.

Nonetheless and unbelievably, we had married by this stage, which seems simply astonishing now that I look back on the events going on around us at the time. Perhaps we both thought that 'tying the knot' would somehow improve our commitment to each other. The wedding itself was a beautiful day, so it seemed like we were off to a good start.

My mother came to Australia for the celebration, which was a huge adventure, considering she had never been on a plane nor travelled outside of the UK before. It was fantastic to see her, and we enjoyed lots of great times together, including the big day itself which I was delighted she could be part of.

Marriage did not improve the underlying flaws in our relationship, and in 1998 Ken and I decided to go our separate ways. Considering how different we are and the way our lives have subsequently been spent, it is perhaps surprising that we stayed together for as long as we did. But, over time as a couple, we had become inextricably linked and probably realised how difficult it would be to untangle that intricate web of a joint life – property, finances and network of mutual friends, not to mention our boys, Jake and Benson.

I reflected fondly on our relationship, during which I enjoyed a deep sense of security with Ken and the comfortable life we'd built together. It was the first time I'd had a proper home to be proud of, and it would be a very long time before I experienced the joy of a real place to call mine again.

Our divorce was relatively straight forward, yet still bruising emotionally, and after 12 years together the 'moving-on' process was a challenging prospect for both of us.

The upside to all of this is that Ken and I have remained the best of friends to this day.

I was in the fortunate position of being able to continue working and support myself financially. But I also realised, with some trepidation, that I was a single woman again, a position I had not been in since my teenage years. And that was a lifetime ago. I was now 41 years old with middle age rapidly approaching.

There is a song that always reminds me of this rather sorrowful era. It talks to the pain of moving forward with simple day-to-day life at the end of a long relationship. Whilst I don't think Ken and I were 'meant' for each other as lifelong partners, we had many loving years together and afterwards it was invariably a time for pondering 'what might have been, could have been, should have been'.

The artist is Jewel from her album 'Pieces Of You', released in 1996.

Playlist Track 13: 'You Were Meant For Me'

# 12

## A Death in the Family

Before progressing to the next stage of my life, I will pause to cover a devastating event that occurred five years earlier when my father passed away.

I have previously written about Dad's difficult childhood. As an adult, he worked long hours in manual jobs and in time managed to set himself up reasonably well financially. However, he was a constant worrier, especially when it came to money and the wellbeing of his family, particularly me and my frequent moves to distant locations. He also experienced stress over circumstances beyond his control, such as global events.

My father was obsessed with saving money. There would never be a light burning in the house for a second longer than absolutely necessary, which meant the family frequently resided in somewhat of a twilight zone. I think he was one of the few people in Britain who was comfortable with the regular blackouts during the 'winter of discontent' strikes in 1978/79 because he realised how much electricity he was saving!

Another of his money-saving tricks was to turn the car engine off at the top of the road to our house, so that he could cruise the rest of the way without consuming petrol. His frugality would drive us all mad at times, especially Mum who was a spendthrift and the complete opposite to Dad.

Yet there was a brief period, during his 40s, when he noticeably chilled out and seemed to enjoy life. He was prepared to frequent the homes of family and friends, take Mum on outings and visit me in London more regularly, even though he usually hated to drive in the city. He really enjoyed coming to Wimbledon when I lived there and my parents spent some happy times at my apartment, so much so that I had difficulty getting them to leave!

My father enjoyed watching practically any sport, a passion he passed on to me. We would spend hours viewing and discussing football, tennis, golf, cricket, athletics and virtually any other sporting event that was being televised. But I did draw the line at boxing and let Dad know he was on his own with that one!

Around the age of 50, I noticed he was once again exhibiting signs of anxiety. Before long, he was taking his obsession with electricity consumption to a whole new level. He took to reading the meter *every* day to monitor how much power was being consumed, which he inevitably felt was too much and would then be even more vigilant about turning off lights and appliances.

Dad had always been a good and careful driver for over 30 years and held a completely clean record – not even a parking fine. He typically ignored and didn't react to anyone on the road who behaved recklessly but, as he grew older, this changed. He became very irate with any driver who might show the slightest hint of aggression and would speed up to confront them, only backing off when my mother or I firmly berated him.

The clearest indicator of there being something seriously amiss with father was in 1989 when I returned after my first spell in Australia. I decided to surprise my parents and had not advised them of my home coming. Mum was over the moon when I appeared unexpectedly, and we had lots to talk about.

But when Dad got back from work, he looked confused when he saw me and asked who I was. Mum gently said, *'Frank, it's our daughter Wendy back from Australia,'* and immediately Dad tried to cover for his temporary loss of memory by laughing it off with a *'Just pulling your leg!'*

I glanced at Mum and could see the concern on her face. Dad was 61 years old at the time.

Over the next two years, my father's mental condition continued to deteriorate but there were also extended periods of time when he seemed fine, hence we all convinced ourselves there was no need to consult a doctor just yet. I was not living at home so didn't witness the worst of his change in behaviour and Mum, God love her, just tried to deal with it alone and not bother me with her worries. Likewise, she said nothing to alarm me when Ken and I announced our plans to return to Australia and our intention to settle in the country long term.

Shortly after we returned to the Gold Coast, Mum told me that Father was getting worse, which culminated later with him being arrested for multiple serious traffic infringements.

Apparently, Dad had taken his car out and was driving continuously around the town's main roundabout in the *opposite* direction to the flow of traffic. Obviously, this caused a fair bit of mayhem, and the police were soon on to him. Dad then proceeded to speed off and out of town, jumping traffic lights on the way.

By then, there was a posse of police vehicles on his tail and eventually they were able to get him to pull over. He refused to get out of the car, so was hauled out, wrestled to the ground, handcuffed and taken back to the police station. By some miracle, my father had not caused an accident or injured anyone and, because he had no previous convictions, was never officially charged for his offences, on the condition that he seek a psychiatric assessment and treatment. His driving licence was however revoked, which shattered him.

The psychiatrist's initial diagnosis was for severe anxiety and depression which was treated with a cocktail of drugs that made my father withdrawn and disinterested in any kind of normal life. The medication was modified but with no real improvement and later, it was determined that Dad had a rare form of early onset dementia called Pick's Disease. It was and remains incurable, and at the time, there was no effective medication to stabilise its symptoms. My mother was told to prepare herself for a fairly rapid decline in his condition.

It was only after my father passed away that Mum filled me in on how awful it had been for her to deal with his ghastly illness. Within a short space of time, my father believed that his wife was actually his mother and failed to recognise my sister or any other family members except Sally's husband. It seemed that, to the very end, Ron was the only person my father could recognise or would co-operate with. Dad refused to interact with anyone else, other than my mother, to whom he became increasingly spiteful and physically abusive.

## A Death in the Family

My father's illness progressed to the point where he declined all food (except *Mars* bars!) and would not wash or go to bed. He spent his days and nights on the sofa vacantly watching television with the sound on high volume. All of which would have been extremely trying for my mother.

The breaking point came when Dad could no longer distinguish between day and night, and he would be found crashing around in the early hours looking for the house keys to go out. One night, Mum came downstairs to find her husband taking a swig from a bottle of bleach which he'd mistaken for a soft drink. Obviously, this situation could not continue, and my mother's doctor insisted she have a period of respite. The medical advice was for father to go into full time care for a few weeks to give mother a break. She was resistant to this but in the end agreed.

My father was picked up the following day and taken to a dementia facility. I didn't know anything about this until I spoke with my mother a few days later for our regular Sunday telephone catchup. She was feeling uncomfortable about 'putting Dad away' but I assured her she had done the right thing; it was only going to be for a short while and would provide her with some much-needed rest. Mum did not give me a full account of the events that unfolded when Dad arrived in care, but she did mention he had a slight chest infection. I felt a sense of foreboding.

I later heard that when my father arrived at the facility, he was completely uncooperative and abusive to staff. Nobody could do anything with him which resulted in my brother-in-law being called in to try and calm the situation. Ron arrived to find Dad naked, huddled in a corner shivering and refusing to move, but he succeeded in getting his father-in-law showered and into bed. That was when Ron noticed Dad's laboured breathing.

The doctor was summoned who diagnosed a chest infection which steadily worsened over the next two days and Dad was hospitalised. He passed away around 24 hours later. My father was only 65 years old when he died.

I received the news in my office at the resort where I was working on the Gold Coast. I realised something was very wrong when the switchboard operator told me she had my brother-in-law on the phone. It was early hours of the morning in Britain, so I knew before Ron spoke that there was some emergency at home and prepared myself for the worse. He broke the news, and my world stopped. I sobbed uncontrollably but managed to thank Ron for what I knew must have been a difficult call for him to make.

The next few days were a whirlwind of making the necessary arrangements to return to the UK. It was just before Christmas, heading into peak season at the hotel and the General Manager was none too thrilled about my absence during a demanding period of business. I promised Johan I would be back as quickly as I could, but right now, he had to give me the time and space I needed.

I was on a flight shortly after the date for Dad's funeral had been established. The question arose about whether Ken would also travel, but I decided it would be better for my mother to have some one-on-one time with me. Additionally, if Ken were to come along, there was the issue of what to do with Benson and Jake, who were just seven months old at the time and still quite a handful.

Upon returning home, I found mother burdened with guilt. I assured her there was no reason to feel guilty, as she had endured so much for so long. I also expressed that Dad's passing was for the best, as he had been deeply unhappy for years with no prospect of an improvement in his health, which had been adversely affecting not only his but her quality of life too. She appeared comforted by my words.

It was a small gathering for Dad's funeral. I thought I would be able to hold things together but struggled with my emotions from the moment I saw the hearse carrying his coffin. A few family members came back to the house for a simple wake of tea and sandwiches. We had some good chats about Dad, focusing on the happier events which marked his days.

I reflected on all the positive ways my father had influenced my life, encouraging me to strive for a good education, fostering an interest in world affairs, nurturing a strong feminist attitude and igniting a passion for a wide range of sports.

Despite these influences, there was something troubling me which I couldn't quite put my finger on. But I do know that as I left my childhood home after my father passed away, a strange sense of relief washed over me. It would be another 10 years before I fully comprehended the source of that relief.

I returned to Australia a few days after the funeral, feeling anguished about not having spent more time with my mother. She was, as ever, so understanding and put no pressure on me to stay... But still, I should have.

I had been absent from work for only just over a week and discovered, on my return, that questions had been raised about the amount of compassionate leave to which I was entitled.

I was hurt and angered by this since I regularly worked additional days without hesitation whenever required, despite the impact of these extended hours on my personal life.

It marked the end of my dedication, and I resigned a year later as by then there was little enthusiasm left for the job, and knew I needed to take a break. This coincided with Ken's parents requiring assistance in their café and I was available to step in.

A few months after leaving the resort, I was astonished to receive a heartfelt letter from Johan, which I have kept to this day. In the note, he expressed how much I was missed and commended me on a job well done.

This uncharacteristic outpouring did make me wonder if, on reflection, Johan had perhaps realised that he could have been more supportive when my father passed away. But I forgave him anyway. My ex-boss went on to play a significant role in shaping my future career path and was instrumental in me securing a brilliant appointment that emerged a few years later.

*This track was included as a late addition after hearing it recently and being immediately reminded of my father. He **loved** Roy Orbison and this song in particular, which was released and became a number one hit in 1964. I'm so happy to have found something appropriate for Dad as an inclusion on my playlist!*

*Playlist Track 14: 'Oh, Pretty Woman'*

## 13

## Reinvention

The personal and professional transformation that took place after the end of my marriage marked a significant mid-life shift for me.

In 1998, I was living in Brisbane with my beautiful golden retrievers and still working in real estate sales. I was once again surprised to receive an unexpected call one day from my old boss Johan who broached the subject of me returning to hotel management. He was involved with a resort further north in Queensland and looking to recruit an Executive Assistant Manager.

My initial reaction was to decline any interest in the role; I had been through enough changes recently, was happy selling real estate and the timing was not right to make another move. But something in my gut told me to at least go and take a look at the property before dismissing it, so I agreed to fly up and find out more.

My initial doubts were confirmed after spending a couple of days at the hotel. It was struggling to attract business and looked a tad rundown. The tropical climate in that part of Queensland was also an issue for me. Jake and Benson would have hated it too.

I called Johan to thank him for thinking of me but advised that I did not wish to be considered for the position.

A few weeks later, another respected veteran of the Australian hotel industry called me from Melbourne. Ralph was known to me by reputation, but we had never crossed paths before.

After introducing himself, Ralph advised that he was also loosely involved with the resort in Queensland, had heard about my recent visit and understood that I was not interested to pursue the opportunity, which I confirmed. I wondered where this conversation was leading and that perhaps he had contacted me to try and change my mind. However, this was not the reason for his call.

Instead, he spoke to me about another property in Sydney which he was working on for the owners. It was a small hotel in The Rocks called *Harbour Rocks Hotel* for which Ralph was recruiting a new General Manager. This was sounding much more interesting – Sydney, The Rocks, small hotel, General Manager. It ticked a lot of boxes.

Soon after, I was back on a plane again, but this time heading south, initially to check out the hotel in Sydney and then fly on to Melbourne for a meeting with Ralph.

*Harbour Rocks Hotel* even back then was a busy and successful property due to its location in the heart of the popular Rocks precinct, adjacent to Sydney Harbour. While it was quite 'tired', the property still retained a certain charm making it popular with tourists from the UK, Europe and USA. I also found it very charming and recognised even greater prospects for its success after a renovation, which was being planned by the owners within the next year or so. I was excited about potentially managing this property and felt it would be worth the effort and stress of uprooting myself and the boys to move interstate.

I travelled on to Melbourne and met Ralph. The recruitment process moved quickly, and I was offered the position at *Harbour Rocks* then and there.

Ralph informed me that he'd known Johan for years and was aware of the high standards expected by my former boss. He was confident I must be a high calibre candidate to have received such a glowing recommendation from Johan, which was good enough to secure me the role. A contract was prepared, and I was pleasantly surprised by its terms – namely, a much higher salary than I'd expected, plus a company car and full relocation expenses.

I was ecstatic on the flight back to Brisbane where I began preparations for the move.

After finding a gorgeous little cottage in Neutral Bay, which was perfect for me and the boys, I happily settled into my new life in Sydney. I drove across the Harbour Bridge every day, which was quite a thrill except when there were four lanes of gridlocked traffic in both directions. On a good day though, I could make the journey to work in around 10 minutes and counted myself extremely lucky to have such an easy commute in a large city.

*Harbour Rocks Hotel* consisted of 55 rooms plus a penthouse suite, a restaurant and bar, a board room for small meetings and six retail tenancies which were on long term leases to independent operators, catering generally to the thriving tourist trade in the area. The property was quite a little gold mine, enjoying occupancies of around 90% year-round. However, I quickly discovered that the level of guest satisfaction was not nearly so healthy as the hotel's level of business.

It was in the days before online feedback platforms such as *TripAdvisor*, which was probably just as well, and the regular flow of complaints I received were by email and letter. The comments related to the poor standard of rooms and how rundown they were, particularly given the premium rates being charged. Fair comment, I thought, so what could we do about this, given that the proposed refurbishment was some way off?

I worked with the housekeeping team to ensure that the property was immaculately presented and set about 'styling' the rooms to improve their presentation. The owners were prepared to spend money on a few cosmetic improvements, and we implemented some cost-effective enhancements to the accommodation.

It's surprising how a lick of paint or new lamps, rugs, cushions, blinds, etc., can enhance a room without incurring a great deal of expense. The Housekeeping Manager, a very capable woman, was so excited by my attention to her area that she quickly had the team on board to lift their game. Apparently, the previous manager had shown little interest in considering minor improvements to the accommodation and was letting things go until a refurbishment was approved.

Once Housekeeping was performing to more exacting standards, I started to work on the receptionists. It appeared to have been some time since anyone had highlighted the service requirements of their role.

## *Reinvention*

One of the major issues was that most clients flew long haul from the northern hemisphere with their flights arriving in Sydney very early in the morning. The guests were exhausted when they arrived at the hotel and were bitterly disappointed to find their rooms were not ready, nor would be for several hours. The best our reception team could offer was, *'Leave your bags and come back at 2pm!'*

I began working on the desk during the busy morning period to roll out improved procedures for dealing with the many early arrivals. I also spoke to the team one-on-one about service expectations in a small property and how we could do things better. I was convinced that if we gave our guests a little more love, they would overlook the tired accommodation. And that was exactly what happened.

The number of complaints received soon reduced to a trickle. The rooms were still basically the same as before but were now being presented in the best light possible. I have always been pedantic about all the little touches in a room being just right as it makes a huge impact on how cared for it presents when a guest first walks in – things like curtains hanging neatly, pictures being straight, beds looking plush, towels folded correctly, armchairs and side tables placed at the correct angle, in room collateral clean and neatly presented... I could go on.

The other big difference was in how the receptionists were by then interacting with guests, from the moment of arrival until the time of departure. The front-line staff were now *engaging* with everyone and making them feel valued instead of just another check-in or check-out. There were some members of the team for whom this improved service culture was too much to take onboard... But they didn't stick around for long.

Throughout 1999, there were high-level changes taking place within the structure of the company which owned *Harbour Rocks* as well as *Hotel Lindrum* in Melbourne and *Cumberland Resort* in Lorne. In due course, a new entity focussing on development was created by parent company and superannuation giant *Cbus*. The new entity was called *Cbus Property* with Kevin Fitzpatrick appointed as its CEO. The three hotels became part of the *Cbus Property* portfolio; therefore, Kevin was my new boss.

Time had moved on during this period of the restructure and there had been other projects at the hotel which required my attention. There were concerns around the potential Y2K problem that loomed with the approach of 31 December 1999, then the introduction of *GST* in July 2000 and the *Sydney Olympics* in September of that year. These events, in addition to the regular daily demands of being a General Manager, meant I had been kept very busy during the two years since starting at *Harbour Rocks*.

The *Olympics* were, of course, huge and an outstanding success for Sydney. The *Games* were great fun to have been involved with and I enjoyed the time immensely, although there were many days when I could barely walk another step by the time I got home after 12-or-more hours running around the hotel. I covered several New Year's Eve's which were always peak periods at *Harbour Rocks* due its location next door to the harbour, but the atmosphere in Sydney for the *Olympics'* closing ceremony was like nothing else I'd previously experienced. It was truly magical.

An amusing incident took place in the hotel during the *Games*. The city was unusually quiet as a big day was scheduled at the Olympic Stadium. Hence, the bar at *Harbour Rocks* was deserted until two respectable looking men arrived and ordered some drinks which they took to a private nook down some steps at the far end of the room.

## *Reinvention*

Shortly afterwards, an attractive young woman arrived and joined the two men. Something felt 'off' to me, and I asked Willie, the barman, to keep an eye on them. In the meantime, I went to interview a prospective Sales Manager in the restaurant, from where I had a partial view of the bar area.

About 20 minutes later, I noticed Willie rush out from behind the bar but didn't think too much of it. I assumed that perhaps the customers wanted to order more drinks, and I carried on with my meeting. Then I was aware of more activity but figured someone would alert me if required, so I proceeded to show the interviewee some hotel rooms.

When I finished, a receptionist informed me that I was needed in the bar area. I went downstairs to find Brenda, the Restaurant Manager, and Willie in fits of laughter. The barman, who was quite a character, told me I'd been spot-on about my hunch with those guests.

Apparently, it had turned into a regular little menage-a-trois on the sofa in that secluded corner of the bar, which resulted in Willie pouncing on them with a soda syphon to cool things down. And this was followed by the three punters scrambling to make their getaway, with one of the guys falling over while trying to run and pull his pants up at the same time. Oh, my goodness!

After the *Games*, it was decided I should move onsite to live in the Penthouse. The apartment had its own entrance at the back of the hotel and a large open-air terrace (with magnificent views of the harbour) which meant there was no issue with Jake and Benson living there with me. Benson, by far the lazier of the two retrievers, was however non-plussed with climbing the 70 steps leading to the accommodation and I'd sometimes find him having a snooze halfway up!

The hotel renovation plans were finalised after the *Olympics* and rolled out during 2001 in small increments so that the property could remain open. This is always a challenge due to disruption caused by the inevitable noise and multiple tradesmen working onsite with their own agendas to manage. I learned a lot during that first major refurbishment in which I was involved, namely that everything is harder, takes longer and is more expensive than originally anticipated!

After several productive and enjoyable years in my first general management position, I began to wonder about prospects for the future. Kevin already had this covered and approached me about taking on a 'group' role, overseeing all three of the *Cbus Property* hotels.

This was a big step-up career-wise and I was flattered that Kevin thought I had the skills for this more senior position in the company. He assumed that I would want to stay in Sydney, and it was planned for my deputy to take over as manager for the day-to-day operations at *Harbour Rocks*, leaving me free to oversee *Hotel Lindrum* in Melbourne and *Cumberland Resort* in Lorne.

Kevin informed me that *The Cumberland* would likely take up most of my time as *Cbus Property* had big plans for the property which they wanted to roll out as soon as possible. After visiting the resort, I realised the scale of these plans and let Kevin know I would prefer to move and be based in Lorne so that I could be on hand to monitor and supervise the project.

Kevin was surprised but happy that I was prepared to move. He had not wanted to make relocation a condition of my promotion as he knew how much I enjoyed living in Sydney but felt far more comfortable with me being onsite in Lorne. My relocation would also make it easier for me to attend regular meetings at *Cbus Property's* office in Melbourne and to oversee *Hotel Lindrum*.

*Reinvention*

And so... Yet another interstate move was imminent. It would wind up impacting my life in many surprising ways, personally as well as professionally. I could not have foreseen just how big that impact would turn out to be.

# 14

## Secrets Shared in San Pedro

In March 2002, I was packing up and preparing for my move to the small regional town of Lorne, regarded as the jewel in the crown of the magnificent Great Ocean Road in Victoria.

Ken helped with the move. He had relocated to Sydney in 2000 with a friend, after both had become disillusioned with their corporate roles in Brisbane. They took a lease on one of the retail spaces at *Harbour Rocks* and opened a coffee shop, so I often had dealings with *'The Latte Brothers'* (which they named their café) and sometimes we socialised together.

As Ken was in Sydney, it was decided that he and I would drive down to Lorne together as that was the easiest way to get my car transported, as well as the boys. It meant I didn't need to put Jake and Benson on a flight again, which had been quite stressful last time around when I moved from Queensland.

On a mild autumn morning, we left Sydney for the 12-hour drive to Lorne. I was moving into the large company house which had been rented by *Cumberland Resort* for several years to accommodate the previous General Manager. It was opposite the beach and had ocean views from virtually every room. The house also had a lovely garden which the resort's maintenance team had fenced in readiness for Jake and Benson's arrival.

The fashionable beachside town of Lorne has many stunning holiday homes owned by wealthy Melburnians which are used for a handful of weekends in the winter and more extensively during the summer months. The climate of Lorne was much cooler than anywhere else I had previously lived in Australia. Jake and Benson must have felt the drop in temperature too as during our first winter there, the boys responded by growing much thicker coats. They transformed into quite the woolly mammoths.

*Cumberland Resort* had been regarded a landmark property in Lorne for decades. The renovations and expansions to the original hotel were centred on timeshare ownership which allowed less affluent Victorians to have a stake in the sought-after location and 'own' an apartment there for a few weeks each year.

This renovation project had apparently been beset with problems and controversy from the beginning, but the revamped and extended resort opened its doors in 1989 with around 100 apartments and had been operating for 13 years by the time I became involved.

Soon after starting work at *The Cumberland*, I quickly realised my engagement represented a significant upheaval for the team. The previous GM had been in the role for around 10 years and virtually all management held similar long-term tenures; hence most staff were understandably concerned about the change in leadership.

After a few weeks, I shared my concerns with Kevin about some of the resistance I was experiencing and how deflated I was feeling. He offered to step in, but I assured him this wasn't necessary, as it might make matters worse. Kevin and I both agreed that if some staff decided to move on this may not be such a bad thing as it would provide an opportunity to introduce fresh energy into the business. Over the following six months, several changes took place which resulted in the appointment of new department heads through a combination of internal promotions and the recruitment of external talent. By then, a team was in place who were ready to handle the transformation being planned for the property.

Lorne can be bleak in winter and unattractive as a holiday destination at that time of year. To attract business in the off-season, a large purpose-built Conference Centre had been constructed as part of the 1989 renovation, which proved to be a successful addition to the resort.

Timeshare had been an innovative model for raising finance to fund the upgrade and extension works back in the 1980s, but it generated very little ongoing operational revenue. By 2003, the business was struggling since conferencing in Lorne had been experiencing a gradual downturn for several years – in part due to newer more modern facilities opening in other attractive regional centres closer to Melbourne.

Since virtually no improvements had been made for over 13 years, the key issue to be addressed when I arrived was that the property urgently required a major facelift. However, many timeshare owners did not have the resources to fund an upgrade and furthermore, were not concerned about their holiday accommodation being rundown since they only spent a few weeks a year there.

But at the same time, *Cbus Property* knew that without the required injection of funds to upgrade the resort, there was no sustainable long-term business. It was clear that moving forward with their plans was going to be a complicated and lengthy process.

Long story short, a year or so later, *Cbus Property* owned enough timeshare units to control the destiny of *The Cumberland*. The costs involved in the 'buy-back' would have been substantial, but ultimately, it was worth this investment to acquire full ownership. It meant that *Cbus Property* would no longer have to deal with a complicated timeshare structure and had complete control over the property. And finally, they were able to push ahead with the resort's renovation.

While plans for the refurbishment – not to mention the many issues involving timeshare owners – took up a good deal of my time, there was still the day-to-day operation to manage along with its ongoing business development activities.

The hotel portfolio's sales and marketing plan for 2003 included a European/UK mission which I was to conduct. *Harbour Rocks* in Sydney already had excellent relations with many oversees operators and we wanted to leverage this strong relationship to drive more international business for *Hotel Lindrum* and *The Cumberland*. The sales trip was planned to take place during the winter off-season when work at *Cumberland* was scheduled to occur, hence the resort would be at low occupancy levels which meant I could be away for a few weeks without any major concerns.

The timing of this happened to coincide with a good friend living in Spain who was turning 40 at the beginning of August and I wanted to join her celebrations. Heidi was the birthday girl, and our mutual friend Colleen was also going to be there. We had all known each other since working together at *Inn on the Park*.

My overseas itinerary included appointments to Australian hotel inbound operators in Germany, Switzerland and Denmark before travelling to Spain for Heidi's 40th. Next stop was London for more sales calls, followed by a week's holiday at home with my mother and then return to Australia.

Ken – yes, he continues to pop up in my story – agreed to look after Jake and Benson in Lorne while I was away. I worked long hours in the lead up, ensuring everything was in place to cover my absence and was relieved to be on my way relaxing in *Singapore Airlines* business class with a glass of champagne. It turned out to be an eventful trip.

I arrived in Frankfurt which, like the rest of Europe in the summer of 2003, was in the midst of a heatwave. Still, I hit the ground running with sales calls in several German cities before moving on to Zurich and Copenhagen. It was an exhausting but successful 10 days during which I was able to generate commitments from most of the operators I visited to feature our Victorian hotels in their following year's Australian programmes.

After the frantic pace of presentations in three countries, I was ready for a break and some downtime with friends in Spain.

I met Colleen, who had just flown in from London, at Malaga airport and we travelled together to San Pedro where Heidi lived. I think both Colleen and Heidi were a little taken aback by how exhausted I looked and commented that I was obviously working way too hard.

After a few days of sun and socialising with my girlfriends, I began to feel like there may indeed be more to life than just work.

As the reader may have gathered by now, I have always been driven career-wise and after my marriage ended, I was even more committed. I had placed my personal life on hold, choosing instead to focus on work and look after my boys. I had been single for five years and, even though still relatively young at 46, held no interest in embarking on another long-term relationship.

While In San Pedro, enjoying the many social activities Heidi had arranged, as well as the laid-back vibe of the pretty little Mediterranean town, I met Jason. He was a friend of Heidi's from London and also visiting as part of a large group invited for the birthday celebrations. He was quite an outspoken individual but there was a definite physical attraction between us. I remember thinking, *'Ah Wendy, perhaps you're not done with men just yet!'*

Jason and I embarked on a holiday romance, which was a significant step for me personally.

After a big night celebrating Heidi's 40th, the following morning dawned typically warm and balmy for that time of year. Jason and I were both nursing hangovers from the excesses of the previous night and enjoying a coffee while chatting together on the roof garden of Heidi's apartment.

Out of the blue, Jason shared with me a very personal secret from his younger days. It was quite a story, and I appreciated his candour in telling me about the circumstances surrounding what had obviously been a devastating event for him.

Then something occurred that I still don't fully grasp. It may have been Jason sharing a sensitive episode from his past but, from somewhere, a deeply buried secret of my own suddenly presented itself with great clarity. I remember saying, *'I guess we all have things that have happened in our lives which we would prefer to forget. For me, it has to do with my father.'*

Those few words triggered recollections that had been lost for years, suddenly appearing in my mind as a series of flashbacks. Tears welled up as I revisited memories long forgotten.

My father's improper behaviour toward me when I was in my early 20's had never been lost in my subconscious, and I later recognised this started at a time when his mental health was deteriorating. He had the early onset of Pick's disease, the symptoms of which can include, in addition to an increasing state of confusion, inappropriate and heightened sexual behaviour.

Dad started following me to the bathroom or would come into my bedroom wanting a hug.

Initially, I thought it was quite sweet as no one in my family was ever openly affectionate with each other. But things started to escalate, and certain situations felt increasingly weird and decidedly uncomfortable.

Then, one morning, Dad got into my bed as I was stirring from sleep and started fondling me. I pushed him away and jumped out of bed as quickly as I could saying, *'Dad, this is not okay.'*

I stormed from the bedroom and locked myself in the bathroom until I heard him go downstairs.

After that, I would avoid being alone with Father and would quiz Mother about her movements for the day so that I could also be out of the house whenever she was absent. I started to find excuses not to go home for extended periods of time during university vacations as I was fearful of getting into situations with my father that I couldn't control. I never really spoke to anyone about this at the time.

Those adult encounters involving my father were one thing, but the flashbacks and outpouring of emotion experienced as I spoke to Jason were nothing to do with these relatively recent situations – they went much further back in time.

I found myself fully present as a four-year-old one Saturday afternoon in the living room of our family home, alone with my father. The weekend was always precious downtime for Dad at the end of a long working week and he loved to catch up with all the sporting action on television. I was playing with my toys in front of the fire when Dad got up and closed the curtains. He then lay down on the sofa and said to me, *'Come lie here with your dad.'*

Innocently, I climbed up on to the sofa. He then started to shuffle around a bit and the next thing I knew, Dad had placed my hand on his penis. Shortly after, following more shuffling around which I didn't understand, Dad told me to go back to my toys.

He said not to mention what had happened and that it would be *'our secret.'*

I do not recall *ever* thinking about it again until that morning in Spain in 2003. It had indeed remained a very well-kept secret... For almost 40 years.

Regardless of what happened, I still believe my father was basically a good man but that he had suffered trauma during his childhood which adversely affected him for his whole life. I think that what he initiated on that Saturday afternoon would have shocked and scared him so much that he resolved it must *never* happen again. Which it didn't, until I was a young woman and Dad was in the throes of a serious mental illness.

I appreciate that in the broader context of sexual abuse, mine was at the milder end of the spectrum. Even so, I believe it has negatively impacted my personal relationships especially around issues of trust.

The recollection of that childhood incident, in addition to the later abuse, made me realise why I often suffered disturbing and recurring dreams. The nightmares usually involved scarily running through a house trying to get away from someone pursuing me or arriving home and being too afraid to enter because I could see a shadow lurking behind the curtains of my bedroom window. I also understood the sense of relief I'd felt when I left home after my father's funeral.

It was the realisation that I would never have to feel afraid of being in that house alone with him again.

I thought that having the childhood trauma resurface and talking about it with Jason and later to Heidi, I had faced it and could move on. But in fact, it was just the beginning. I tried to come to terms with what had happened, however it wasn't until a few years later that I sought and received the psychological help I needed.

I left Spain in a dazed state but still had the UK leg of my trip to complete. After sales calls in London, I spent some time with my mother. It was almost seven years since Dad passed away and Mum seemed happy and settled. She had thought about moving house for a fresh start after she was widowed, but instead had completed renovations on the family home – something she had always wanted to do. My mother had done a lovely job on the house, and the make-over of several rooms also meant I was reminded less of what had happened there in the past.

I caught up with Jason again in London before returning to Australia, and we continued to stay in touch for a while. I do have to say 'thank you' to Jason... wherever he may now be. Our holiday romance and opening up to him shifted my outlook on life. I felt different, somehow lighter and more liberated by the end of that short time in San Pedro.

When I returned to Lorne, it was a very different Wendy who arrived back in town. The protective wall I had built around myself for years was not completely broken down, but it had certainly been broached. I was also able to entertain the idea that I was still reasonably attractive. The realisation of this made me more confident in the way I started to dress and behave, particularly around men.

*The Cumberland's* renovation had been progressing well while I'd been overseas but, as usually happens, there had been some complications along the way, and it would be another couple of months before everything was finished.

The lead construction company was doing an excellent job but were concerned about how hard their various trades were being pushed to keep the project on target for a pre-Christmas completion, ready for the resort's busy summer season. It was felt that a little morale boost was needed to keep the team on side for a timely completion of the work.

## Secrets Shared in San Pedro

A date was set for a barbecue to be hosted at the resort, in appreciation of all the efforts to date and as an incentive to maintain the tight timeline moving forward. The event began just after lunch, and everyone had a fine old time with a fair amount of drinking throughout the afternoon. Later, a group of us took the party over to *Lorne Hotel*. By around 8pm, I decided it might be time for me to call it a day.

For some insane reason, I decided to go pick up my car from the resort and, on the way, bumped into a man I knew who I'd met fleetingly on several previous occasions. Sam suggested I was in no fit state to drive, and that he would take me.

'And you think you're in better shape?' I laughed. 'Please don't worry about it, I live literally just up the road.'

Nevertheless, he insisted, and we wound up sharing a brief kiss on my driveway. Fortunately, Sam's mobile started to ring incessantly which dampened the mood and we decided it best he go back to the pub and show his face to avoid any uncomfortable questions being raised about where he had been. Sam said he would return as soon as he could... *Really?*

I was obviously more intoxicated than I thought because the next thing I knew, it was the following morning. I awoke feeling somewhat 'foggy' but could recall some inappropriate behaviour on my part. Oh my God, what had I done exactly?

I kicked back the doona and saw that I was looking perfectly respectable in my pyjamas, *'Oh, maybe not so bad after all,'* I thought. I checked out Jake and Benson who were still snoozing in the bedroom and was horrified to think that I had gone to bed without feeding them. However, I checked the kitchen and found their empty food bowls on the floor, so I had obviously fed them before crashing out. Ok, so far, so good... But then I checked my phone and discovered the many missed calls from Sam throughout the course of the previous evening. I quickly pulled my mind into gear and remembered that there had been 'something' between us, but nothing more than that. I prayed that Sam had not and would not mention anything to anyone about what had taken place between us.

Later that day, I called Sam in Melbourne and apologised for my inappropriate behaviour the night before. He assured me that all was well, I had nothing to apologise for and that it would remain between the two of us. Thank you!

I tentatively probed the resort team for any gossip that might be circulating involving me from the night of the barbecue, but there was no word of anything untoward. It looked like my reputation remained intact! There were in fact a few positive comments about it being good to see me socialising and enjoying myself out-and-about in Lorne for once.

A week or so later, Sam called to ask if he could book a room for the following Sunday night as he had a meeting in town early Monday morning. I thought it was kind of odd that he hadn't simply gone through the Reservations department at the resort to make his booking. It crossed my mind that perhaps Sam wanted me to know he was going to be staying overnight in Lorne in a few days' time.

It was cold and raining on that Sunday in late September, so I had been enjoying a quiet day relaxing by the fire at home with my boys. I received a call from Sam in the afternoon to ask if I wanted to join him and his friends for dinner. I declined the invitation but did say he was welcome to come and have a drink with me before or after dinner if he wished.

Without any hesitation, Sam said that he would pop up to the house after dinner. When I hung up, I threw my phone along the kitchen bench, berating myself and wondering what I was thinking by making such a foolish proposal. But I didn't call back to cancel the invitation.

I thought I'd better tidy myself up a bit, but figured there was plenty of time before Sam was likely to show up after his dinner. I was only just ready and surprised when there was a knock on my front door.

*'Wow, he's keen,'* flashed through my mind. The boys were excited, as always with visitors, and welcomed our guest enthusiastically. I could see that Sam wasn't used to being around dogs, but he did his best to look comfortable with my two enormous over affectionate golden retrievers.

Sam and I sat at opposite ends of my large sofa in front of the open fire and by now a very wintry night had settled in outside. It was warm and cosy inside, and I poured us some red wine. I'd already had a couple of glasses to steady my nerves as it had been some time since I'd invited a man to my house.

Years of being in hotel management has made it relatively easy for me to make small talk and put people at ease, and this was no different. I asked Sam about himself. He told me he had completed his degree two years ago and after some overseas travel had accepted a role in his chosen field.

I remember thinking, *'He finished university only a couple of years ago?!'*

That would make him a whole lot younger than I'd assumed. Based on the maturity with which he conducted himself and his confidence in the few conversations I'd had with him, not to mention our 'encounter' of the previous week, I thought he was aged around 30.

As I write this, more than 20 years later, I can still see Sam in my sitting room in Lorne and listening to him talk, wondering where this was all leading. Because sure as hell, it was leading somewhere.

Sam didn't need the room I'd booked for him at the resort that night.

Before leaving the following morning, I casually enquired about his age.
'23,' he chirpily responded.
Err right, so after completing a mental back flip, I continued, 'And so... How old do you think I am?'
'Oh, I think you'd be a bit older.'
'Like what?'
'Ooh, about 36?' (Bless!)
'Hmmm, try adding another decade.'
'No way, you're kidding me!'
'True about the age, I'm afraid. Wouldn't be overstating it, given the current circumstances.'
Silence. Then, after doing the maths, I had an awful thought, 'Oh, dear God, don't tell me I'm older than your mother?'
'Don't be silly, not even close!'

It turned out to be *very* close in fact!

And so began the unlikeliest of relationships. I was attracted to Sam but from the outset knew this was going to be a tricky affair to navigate due to our age difference.

However, for now I was very cheerful because Sam quickly became a welcome diversion from some of the darker thoughts which had been manifesting during my time in Lorne.

From the start, I had felt isolated and alone in such a small country town and, at some point, began to consider the notion of not being around anymore. After all, I wasn't a big enough part of *anyone's* life to be missed – I had one parent on the other side of the world, no partner or children and only a few close friends.

Nobody really except for Jake and Benson, and their unconditional love meant I could not leave them. But my boys were getting older so perhaps it would only be a matter of time before they too were no longer a consideration. My time overseas had definitely given me something of a new lease on life, but I was also grappling with the memories that had resurfaced on that trip, and it was only after I started seeing Sam that the clouds in my head truly began to lift.

The next few months were a whirlwind of finishing the renovation works and planning *Cumberland's* relaunch... as well as secret rendezvous with Sam.

The transformation of the resort was sensational and a rewarding outcome for all concerned. The team at *Cumberland* had gone from strength to strength in the last 12 months with old faces doing great jobs in new roles and fresh recruits bringing good ideas and enthusiasm into the business.

I felt proud for all that had been achieved and for the resilience I had shown after such a discouraging start to my tenure at the resort. The relaunch party in the newly revamped restaurant on a summer's evening in January 2004 was a huge success. The whole project team was in attendance along with many executives from *Cbus Property* and its parent company *Cbus*, senior management from each of the hotels, as well as major clients which included conference organisers, inbound operators and travel writers.

## *Life for Rent*

I had survived many challenges in two years at the helm of the resort and now it was time to move on to Melbourne. *Hotel Lindrum* had been very successful in the five years since it opened but there were some ongoing issues at the property which Kevin wanted me to oversee now that *The Cumberland* was finished.

A week or so after the relaunch party, I was packing up the house in Lorne and heading to Albert Park, a fashionable inner-city bayside suburb of Melbourne. The move, I hoped, would mean I might see more of Sam as my relocation meant we would both have our home and work bases in the same city.

In 2003, The Rolling Stones embarked on a world-wide tour celebrating their incredible 40 years together. I had never seen the rock legends live but that year I made up for it by attending three of their concerts — in Sydney, Melbourne and London. So, it would be remiss of me for this chapter to overlook one of their big numbers which featured prominently in all their shows.

Playlist Track 15: 'Honky Tonk Women'

And for a complete change of pace but also from 2003 when a young British artist, Katie Melua, released her successful debut album 'Call Off the Search'. The album's first single takes me back to the early days of my relationship with Sam and some of the lyrics resonate with emotions I felt at the time.

Playlist Track 16: 'The Closest Thing to Crazy'

## 15

## Magic Tragic Melbourne

In February 2004, the boys and I set up house in Melbourne and it would be the final move Jake and Benson made. They enjoyed the last four years of their lives with me in a Victorian terrace on Richardson Street, a short walk to the cafes and shops of Albert Park Village.

My new home was close to the city where *Hotel Lindrum* was situated on Flinders Street. The property was a convenient location for business travellers as well as leisure guests, being a stone's throw from the *Melbourne Cricket Ground (MCG)* and *Rod Laver Arena*, both of which host major sporting events for which the city is famous.

The hotel was also adjacent to the city's business district, Southbank arts precinct, Melbourne's theatre district, as well as the upmarket shops and restaurants 'at the Paris end' of Collins Street.

*Hotel Lindrum* was a heritage building originally the site of *Griffiths* tea and coffee merchants. It later became *Lindrum's Billiards Centre*, managed by Dolly who was the niece of former world champion Walter Lindrum.

I discovered that Dolly lived just around the corner from me in Albert Park and I visited her on a regular basis – she was a charming woman. The billiard hall had been closed for several years and the building had fallen into disrepair before its owners had the vision to develop the space and transform it into a luxury boutique hotel. They also spent time with Dolly during the redevelopment of the site to ensure that the building's historic links to billiards were featured in the new design.

Dolly was elated when she heard that the property was to be called *Hotel Lindrum* and that there would be a full-size billiards table as a centre piece in the bar area on the ground floor.

The hotel was officially opened to great fanfare in 1999 by then Victorian Premier Jeff Kennett. With its understated elegance, *Hotel Lindrum* encapsulated the essence of Melbourne and enjoyed success from day one. The building was striking with its neo-Romanesque heritage façade and the refurbishment had been carried out with meticulous attention to detail.

*Hotel Lindrum* was small with just 59 rooms but never failed to impress with its classic yet contemporary style. It was once described by a travel journalist as *'ideal for the aspiring groovy couple.'* (Mary O'Brien, The Sydney Morning Herald Lifestyle/Travel, 'Have a ball in old billiard hall', June 2006)

The property flourished in the early 2000s when there was a definite shift in demand with guests seeking more authentic experiences in their lodging choices, moving away from the bland uniformity of large chain brands.

## Magic Tragic Melbourne

Boutique hotels became very fashionable, and the *Australian Hotels Association (AHA)* introduced a category in their annual awards to recognise this emerging style of accommodation. In 2002, *Hotel Lindrum* won the category for 'Best Boutique Hotel in Australia'. It was a tremendous accolade, and I was thrilled to share in the celebrations at the national awards held on the Gold Coast.

As Group General Manager, I had been closely involved with the *Lindrum* since it opened and was familiar with its operation, however, had not been based there until 2004 when I moved to Melbourne.

By then, several maintenance issues could no longer be ignored, and it was determined that a mini facelift was required to the rooms and public spaces. *Cbus Property* had been impressed with the construction company on the Lorne project who were subsequently appointed for the work at *Lindrum*.

The hotel re-launched a few months later looking even more fabulous than when it opened. Business was booming, hotels having recovered from the post-9/11 slump, with domestic as well as international visitor numbers rebounding strongly. And everyone, it seemed, wanted to stay in trendy boutique hotels. *The Lindrum's* reputation continued to soar along with its occupancy and room rates. Happy days!

My personal life, however, was not proceeding quite so successfully...

The relationship with Sam was not really going anywhere as neither of us wanted to 'come out' about it due to that 'little' issue relating to our respective ages. I had told a few trusted friends and Sam likewise, but we didn't socialise with any of them initially. Sam's family were also unaware, as they would certainly have had an expectation to meet their son's girlfriend. And for obvious reasons, Sam was not keen for this to happen any time soon.

Therefore, to all appearances, Sam lived the life of a single young man in Melbourne and was quite the social butterfly. Even so, he would spend a night or two each week at my place. This continued for about a year and although we gradually started to socialise with friends, I felt very insecure in our relationship.

A few in Sam's circle were accepting of me but others deemed that our romantic involvement was highly inappropriate. My friends were far more tolerant with a 'go girl' attitude to the whole situation. I understood those who held a negative opinion, but it did make me reflect on the taboo and double standards around older women/younger men compared to the acceptance of men in relationships with much younger women. I realised that societal norms were not going to change any time soon, so had to accept that both Sam and I would face criticism from some quarters by our decision to be together.

We continued to drift in and out of an on again, off again liaison until the middle of 2005. In July that year, I attended the General Manager's summer programme at *Cornell University's School of Hotel Administration* in America. It was something I'd had on my radar for years and *Cbus Property* agreed to finance the course.

I decided to take some leave after the two-week course at *Cornell* in upstate New York and headed over to Italy where I spent time in Venice and Florence, enrolled in cooking classes in Tuscany and then headed down to Positano on the Amalfi Coast, where my friend Colleen joined me from London for a few days.

It was a superb trip from beginning to end which I could write a whole chapter about but instead just mention here in context to how its timing and the weeks I spent overseas shifted the dynamics of the relationship between Sam and myself.

When I returned to Melbourne, we caught up for lunch and, while Sam seemed glad to see me, I could sense that something was pre-occupying him. When we were about to leave the restaurant he said, *'I've got something to tell you.'*

I was correct in thinking that I knew what was coming. Sam had met someone while I'd been away, and things were apparently going well so understandably he could no longer see me. I was quite devastated but tried to remain composed and understanding. And truly, I did completely get that Sam needed to pursue a romantic involvement with someone his own age. And yet I knew he still had feelings for me, as I did for him. We parted company, wishing each other well. There had previously been times when one or other of us would say we *'can't do this anymore,'* but a few weeks later, the relationship would be back on again. This time was different though because Sam was now seeing someone else on a serious basis.

In the months that followed, I was quite a mess emotionally. I ate too little, drank too much and generally felt depressed, but somehow managed to hold myself together. I would find all sorts of reasons to call Sam, and he always remained patient and friendly with me.

His company began work on a project conveniently located next door to *Hotel Lindrum* and one evening I decided to stop by and say hello. The chemistry was still there between us and once again we resumed our romance. Just one small problem though… Sam seemed reluctant to let go of the 'other' girlfriend.

After a few weeks of this, my self-respect kicked in and I issued an ultimatum. I let Sam know that our secretive affair could not continue. I was prepared to give our relationship a real chance, but only if he felt likewise. This meant telling his family and friends so that we could socialise openly like any other normal couple. And, needless to say, he had to end his involvement with the current girlfriend.

I really wasn't sure how Sam would react to my demands but was adamant that enough was enough and this time it had to be all or nothing. Somewhat surprisingly, he agreed with me. Thus, more than two years after first becoming involved with each other, we finally said, *'Let's do this!'*

Sam had the conversation with his parents and, while there were probably some concerns raised, they kept an open mind to our relationship and were extremely welcoming towards me. In time, I met his extended family and enjoyed all their regular gatherings and celebrations.

Over the next few years, Sam and I had many special times together. Whether it was simply watching our beloved *Bombers* (we both supported Aussie-rules team *Essendon*) in the stands of the *MCG* or dining out at smart restaurants in Melbourne or attending concerts and the theatre, we enjoyed the occasions as well as each other's company immensely.

We travelled interstate extensively and managed to fit in several trips internationally to New Zealand, Bali, Greece, Turkey and the UK. I think one of the reasons we packed so much into our relatively short time together was that subconsciously we both knew our relationship would reach a tragic inevitability.

Tragedy did indeed strike in March 2007. However, neither Sam nor I could have foreseen that this shocking event would also mark the beginning of the end to our time together.

The ongoing success and popularity of *Hotel Lindrum* had led to discussions with Kevin about the feasibility of extending the hotel's concept and opening properties of a similar style in all the major capitals of Australia. *Cbus Property* were developing a site at the top end of Bourke Street in Melbourne which was going to be a larger version of the original *Lindrum* and would be called *Lindrum on Bourke*.

There were also plans for a major facelift to *Harbour Rocks* in Sydney to give it more of a *Lindrum* feel. Once these two projects were completed, it was envisaged to extend the brand to Brisbane, Adelaide, Canberra and Perth, whenever development opportunities presented themselves in those cities.

It was an exciting prospect and during 2006, I became increasingly involved in the design plans for *Lindrum on Bourke*. I was still responsible for the day-to-day running of *Hotel Lindrum* as its General Manager, while also overseeing *Harbour Rocks* and *The Cumberland*. Kevin felt I was spreading myself too thinly and now insisted, as had been his plan from the outset, that I have a Hotel Manager in each property so that the daily operations were delegated to another appropriate senior person, leaving me with more time for new projects. This meant I needed to recruit a manager for *Hotel Lindrum*.

On Monday 5 March 2007 at 4pm, I had an appointment with Kevin in his office for one of our regular catchups. I planned to let him know that I'd made an offer to a candidate which had been accepted for the management role at *Lindrum*, which I knew Kevin would be very happy about.

When I arrived in the foyer of the company's office in Collins Street, I was met by the Chief Financial Officer. He was visibly shaken as he took me aside to break the news that Kevin had suffered a heart attack a few hours earlier and couldn't be revived. He had passed away in his office. Kevin was only 58 years old.

The sudden loss of our beloved CEO in such tragic circumstances hit everyone in the company hard. Not only was Kevin a very competent leader, but he was also a genuinely lovely person. Most of us had been working with Kevin for several years and had tremendous respect and affection for him.

There was a large gathering for his funeral at Ripponlea, which Sam and I attended, where many people spoke beautifully of their memories of Kevin. None more so than his wife Chris, who managed to remain composed despite her obvious and intense grief.

I have stayed in touch with Chris since then and it's always a pleasure when we find ourselves in the same city, to catch up over lunch or dinner. Whenever we meet, I always sense that Kevin is never far from Chris's thoughts, despite the number of years which have passed since that awful day in 2007.

Gradually, life and work returned to normal, and a new CEO for *Cbus Property* was appointed from one of the company's existing executives.

By the end of the year, it was becoming evident that Kevin's vision for extending the *Lindrum* brand throughout Australia would not come to fruition.

In fact, it had been decided that all the hotel assets were to be sold and there would be no further development of existing sites!

This news was a great shock to me. I understood the reasons why and that running hotels was not part of the company's core business, but the revelation turned my life upside down. As 2007 drew to a close, I had a good deal to think about.

I made the decision to move on after the hotels were sold. Almost 10 years had passed since I joined the company and it had been very satisfying, but the prospect of transitioning the hotels to new owners did not excite me. I was asked to stay on to complete due diligence during the sale process because of my intimate knowledge of each property. In return, *Cbus Property* offered me a generous redundancy package and we set the end of the financial year as my termination date.

Over the summer, Sam and I spent some time on the Sunshine Coast with his parents. The boys were looked after by a couple of different work colleagues who, over the years, had always taken it in turns to spend time at the house dog sitting whenever I was away.

On returning home, it was apparent to me how much Jake and Benson had slowed down in the last few months. They were both starting to really struggle with their joints and didn't want to walk far. Jake was virtually deaf, and his vision was also fading while Benson was generally cranky much of the time.

Reluctantly, I said to them, *'Oh my darling boys, I think you've had enough, haven't you?'*

I spoke to the vet about my concerns, and he agreed that the time had probably come to let them go with dignity and without any possible suffering.

It was quite the final week for my boys, enjoying all their favourite food as well as many friends visiting and making a big fuss of them. Sam's mother organised a barbecue on Jake and Benson's last night, which was so sweet of her, knowing how much the boys would love to share in the tasty dinner. She was also aware of how I was struggling to get through this difficult period and that I needed plenty of support.

I took the day off work and spent it with my boys having little walks and lots of cuddles. I had determined they would not endure the additional stress of a last visit to the vet's surgery and instead remain in their own familiar surroundings.

The vet arrived at 6pm and he could not have been more caring and compassionate. It was still awful, of course, and the hardest thing I've ever had to do in my life. I wanted my beautiful 'goldens' to go to sleep with me massaging their furry bodies, which they adored, and quietly repeating how much I loved them. Which is exactly what I did until the vet checked their hearts for the final time and said, *'Wendy, your boys have passed away peacefully.'*

And you know what? They did indeed look way more peaceful than I had seen them in a while. It was 6 February 2008, three months before their 15th birthday – a very good innings for two large dogs, but their long lives did not make it any easier for me to handle. I was totally broken and felt like I was drowning in the flood of my own tears. And I'm not a teary person, as anyone who knows me will vouch for.

Sam was as supportive as knew how to be, but I don't think he really understood the depth of my grief. He and I had a walking holiday booked to the Queen Charlotte Pass in New Zealand with friends the following week. It helped settle me to be physically active surrounded by caring people amongst nature in the breathtaking beauty of the country's South Island.

Back in Melbourne, the hotel sales were proceeding, and I needed to start thinking about another position. There were a couple of openings in Melbourne but nothing that really appealed. I began to consider options further afield since I was no longer limited to locations which were suitable for Jake and Benson. Sam was alarmed when I brought this up as he had assumed that our life together would continue in Melbourne.

I broached the subject of perhaps it was the right time to think about moving on, but Sam insisted that this was not what he wanted, and we could work things out even if our relationship became long distance. I felt confused and conflicted by the events of the last few months so agreed with him, as deep down I didn't want to break up either.

At the same time, I felt that if not now, then when?

We had already attended the weddings of a few of Sam's friends, and some of them had gone on to start a family. This was never going to happen for Sam if he remained living with me and I wondered how long it would be before he craved a more normal life.

We carried on but, after the announcement of my redundancy and the passing of Jake and Benson, there was a heaviness between us which didn't exist previously. Changes were coming, which neither he nor I could alter… Or perhaps we just didn't have sufficient desire to do so.

My last day of work wound up being in July 2008 and I was given a farewell party at the *Press Club* bar next door to *Hotel Lindrum*. *Cumberland's* General Manager drove up from Lorne with several of his team, which had remained pretty much unchanged since the time when we had assembled it six years previously.

The manager at *Harbour Rocks* flew down from Sydney and everyone from *Hotel Lindrum* attended. I looked around feeling very proud of the array of talent we had in the room that night and sorry that this group was being gradually disbanded as the sale of each property completed. It had been a privilege to have worked with countless fine individuals for so many years.

I gave a speech based around people asking me which had been my preferred hotel. I felt it was rather like asking a parent which was their favourite child! I described *Harbour Rocks* as the charismatic kid who charmed everyone, *Hotel Lindrum* as the good-looking younger sibling who didn't have to work too hard to get on in life and *Cumberland* as the naughty, troublesome one who came good in the end!

The following day, I returned to my office to pick up the last of my belongings and tie up a few loose ends. I felt incredibly emotional leaving that office for the last time with some extraordinary memories from the last 10 years. It was, and would remain, my longest tenure by far with any employer.

I had not appreciated quite how much of a toll on my mental wellbeing the previous six months had taken. But I did know that I needed to get away for a few weeks and spend some time alone interspersed with seeing family and friends.

So, I headed back to the UK to see my mother and old school chums Anne and Deborah, as well as Colleen in London. I returned to Spain and visited Heidi again, then dropped into Vietnam on my way back to Australia to see Brenda, who I'd worked with at *Harbour Rocks*. She was by then working as a hospitality teacher for disadvantaged young people in a not-for-profit organisation in Hanoi. It was a rejuvenating trip, and I returned with some clarity around what I wanted to do next.

## Magic Tragic Melbourne

In the months leading up to my redundancy, I had been in discussions with *Voyages Resorts* who were keen for me to consider managing one of their luxury properties, all of which were located in remote locations. And all of them a long way from Melbourne...

> Note: The three hotels with which I was closely involved from 1998-2008 have changed hands again since they were sold during my time at *Cbus Property*. *Harbour Rocks Hotel* and *Cumberland Resort* continue to operate as up-market boutique hotels and are managed by separate entities. Sadly, *Hotel Lindrum* no longer exists – it closed recently and the whole site is undergoing redevelopment, scheduled for completion in 2026. It will be interesting to see the property's next reincarnation!

There are many songs which take me back to this astonishing 10 years of my life, and I've had to cull the list considerably to include only two.

The first was released in 1999, so a bit before the specific era covered in this chapter, but it always makes me think of Hotel Lindrum. A receptionist used to play the album on rewind until one day a colleague had enough and destroyed it! Shame, because I rather liked 'Rise' by British singer Gabrielle and include the title track here.

Playlist Track 17: 'Rise'

The second is at last an inclusion on my playlist from George Michael! It's the hit single from his

2004 album 'Patience' which was a favourite with both Sam and me. A great song from a greatly missed artist.

Playlist Track 18: 'Amazing'

# 16

## Lizard Island

---

I had thought about the possibility of managing a remote exclusive island destination for some time and in September 2008, the opportunity to do so materialised. Part of the allure would have been fond memories of working on Paxos all those years ago, however Lizard Island turned out to be a somewhat different experience.

It *certainly is* a remote destination! The flight from Melbourne to Cairns takes three-and-a-half-hours. The journey continues by transferring to a small 12-seater aircraft for the scenic one hour crossing over the Great Barrier Reef to Lizard Island. When you factor in transfers to and from the various airports, it's a full day of travel that's involved. Sam and I discussed the logistics of how we might manage this and still be able to see each other regularly. We thought it was doable by each of us alternating the trip and spending a few days together in either Melbourne or Lizard Island every few weeks. What could possibly go wrong?

During the interview process I visited the resort and, even at that stage, had concerns about what I was letting myself in for as its General Manager. The property was in the process of being sold by *Voyages*, along with most of their portfolio around Australia.

*Delaware North* was the eventual purchaser of *Lizard Island Resort,* plus several other sites in the *Voyages* collection. Given the uncertainty of future ownership and what that might mean for the tenure of its General Manager, in addition to the isolation of the location, there was a limited number of suitable candidates who expressed interest in taking on the role.

The relatively insecure situation actually suited my circumstances. Sam and I had talked about taking a year off work in the foreseeable future to spend time in Europe so were comfortable with making the commitment to a long-distance relationship for up to 12 months, during which time we could formalise our plans for an extended period overseas. It would also acquaint me with managing a remote property and see how it suited, as well as allowing Sam to successfully complete the current projects he was working on in Melbourne. Therefore, we had a plan which, we hoped, would keep us both sufficiently motivated to make the time apart work.

*Lizard Island* was, and still is, regarded as one of the premier retreats in Australia. The only buildings on the island are the resort and a marine research station. Its position on the far reaches of the Great Barrier Reef mean it is blessed with pristine water and beaches.

The resort has 40 villas dotted around a semi-circle of white sand overlooking the magnificent Coral Sea. Lizard Island's distance from the mainland allows its surrounding waters to remain free of stingers which plague the rest of North

## *Lizard Island*

Queensland. Stingers are potentially lethal jelly fish which make the sea too dangerous in which to swim at many of the state's coastal locations during summer.

The waters surrounding *Lizard* are warm, soft and crystal clear all year round, teaming with colourful marine life as well as spectacular coral. And there are no pesky jelly fish to worry about!

Guests staying at the resort did so on an all-inclusive basis meaning that breakfast, lunch and dinner were provided along with a generous beverage allowance which included *Louis Roederer* champagne. Well, with rates starting at $1,500 a night (back then, 15 years ago) one might expect a bit more than just a room with a view!

Other facilities available included an extensive water sports department offering private boats to secluded beaches as well as snorkelling, scuba diving and deep-sea fishing. There was also a rather fabulous day spa offering an array of pampering treatments.

It all sounds pretty amazing, right? Not really…

When I arrived to start my new role, I was surprised by how the property presented. The villas were in reasonable condition, but I felt that the public areas looked below par.

I shared some of my observations and concerns with the team at our daily management meetings, which did not go down too well with most of them, but interestingly, some of the others appreciated my 'back to basics' approach.

In retrospect, I should have handled things differently to get the group more on side during my first weeks which would have made life easier. Instead, the directness resulted in a fair amount of negativity which was not conducive to me settling into the new position, and particularly challenging in a location where everyone is living as well as working together. I was also heavily criticised for not socialising with the team in the staff bar and could have made more of an effort on that front too.

But, after working at least 12 hours each day in a very hands-on role and playing 'mine host' for up to 80 guests, the last thing I felt like doing was having drinks with staff, because effectively I was still on duty. However, I should have set a night or two aside each week and made more time for the team in a social setting. After an enjoyable life in Melbourne with a wide circle of friends, I quickly began to feel the isolation of being General Manager on *Lizard Island*.

There were clients who would say how lucky they thought I was to live in such idyllic surroundings, but the reality was that as soon as I walked out of the house each morning, my every move was observed by guests and staff alike. It felt like being the star of a show I didn't want to be performing in, constantly monitored to do and say the right thing with no down time. Exhausting! I was ready to call it quits after the first month, but Sam persuaded me to persevere for a bit longer, knowing that I would be disappointed in myself should I give up so quickly, and he was right. I resolved to carry on and see how things were panning out after three months.

Over the next few weeks, I continued working on the property and acquired some funds from *Voyages* to make a few cosmetic improvements. Slowly but surely, the resort began, in my opinion, to look better.

I was also learning more about the back-of-house workings of the property, which were complex due to its location. The resort generated its own electricity, treated all sewage, purified its water and had to be self-sufficient in all the utilities one normally takes for granted on the mainland. This necessitated a reasonably large engineering team on site to keep all these processes compliant and functioning, as well as handling the numerous day-to-day maintenance issues.

It was an enormous challenge in an ageing property, but the guys did a good job staying on top of things – even though most of them were first to arrive and last to leave the staff bar each night!

The majority of supplies came by barge once a fortnight from Cairns, and this was always a big day for the resort when everything from fuel to food, new equipment to spare parts, and everything in between would arrive.

If anyone forgot to order something, there would be two more weeks to wait before the next barge arrived, which meant all departments needed to efficiently manage their stock and purchasing processes. There was also a cargo plane which delivered perishables and urgent items to *Lizard* several times a week, however this was an expensive means of transportation. The frequency of these flights was therefore kept to a minimum and generally only utilised for the delivery of fresh food items.

Staff turnover was high when I joined *Lizard Island* but in time, it improved dramatically. I can partly attribute this to firmly setting the ground rules, calling out inappropriate behaviour and removing those responsible from the island, which in turn encouraged good employees to remain. This resulted in a more cohesive and engaged team who worked on the island for longer and turnover was reduced, along with all its associated costs.

Now, I love a glass of wine or two as much as most people in hospitality but was concerned that so many of the staff activities revolved around the bar and consumption of alcohol. I decided we needed a think-tank about how to introduce some healthier team building options.

We came up with a simple plan to make up four teams from all the employees on the island and mix them up between the different departments. This meant staff were with individuals from other areas who they may not regularly work or socialise with.

We devised a programme of events with points and prizes awarded accordingly. There were lots of sporting activities, but also quiz and trivia nights, cooking competitions, bake-offs, clean-up working bees and anything else we could think up to involve the skills and interests of as many employees as possible.

Virtually everyone bought into the competition far more enthusiastically than I could have imagined! There was much excitement as to who was on which team, what their team's name would be and selecting captains.

It all proved to be great fun, and a healthy rivalry developed between the teams. While it's true that many of the activities were followed by a celebratory session in the bar, which I usually joined in, drinking had not been the main reason for staff to interact with each other.

There were positive steps being made in some aspects of my role, but the restaurant remained a particular challenge for me to overcome. The variety and quality of food produced by the kitchen brigade was generally top notch, however there were issues regularly raised relating to inconsistencies in standards of service delivery.

## Lizard Island

The Restaurant Manager had been supportive of me when I arrived and also very honest about the problems in her department, so I wanted to help. I began by spending as much time as I could working in the restaurant during meal periods, but this was obviously not sustainable long term. After several weeks of my providing hands-on support, the manager felt her department was improving. But I was not totally convinced of this. So, it seemed likely I would need to continue overseeing the restaurant for a fair bit longer.

But what was I still doing there? Had I not been planning to most likely quit after three months?

Well... Sam had managed a couple of trips to *Lizard* but, to be honest, his visits were always quite tense as he, not unreasonably, expected more of my time than I was able to give. When I was on the island, guests expected me to be playing host to their needs and didn't appreciate that I might be taking a day off. Even though I may have worked non-stop for several weeks leading up to a visit from Sam, the current group of guests did not of course factor this into why I was not always available and playing host to them for the duration of *their* stay.

The Rooms Division Manager would step up when I took time off, but it didn't matter because guests would see me at leisure around the island; in such a small place it was impossible not to be seen out and about, and many did not understand the concept of a GM having days off. There was even some feedback posted online at one point which I was most upset about, *'The General Manager spent more time with her boyfriend than attending to the resort guests.'*

It became clear that if I was physically present on the island, I was effectively on duty 24/7.

After a busy Christmas and New Year period, the resort settled into lower occupancies with the onset of the rainy season in tropical North Queensland. I took this opportunity to return to Melbourne for a much-needed break at the end of January 2009 and to reassess with Sam my timeline for remaining at *Lizard*.

He and his parents were planning to visit the island in March, and I had also booked the two of us in for a few nights at *El Questro* in the *Kimberlies* during April. We decided that I would resign when I returned to *Lizard*, giving three months' notice which meant I would leave at the end of April.

My resignation was reluctantly accepted by the Regional General Manager who requested the news remain confidential until nearer the time of my departure. I was asked to consider staying on for a bit longer otherwise my boss would have to hold the fort on *Lizard* until after the sale of the resort, which was looking likely to settle around the middle of the year.

It was a relief to have decided about my future. And, with a definite date now set for a return to Melbourne, Sam and I settled into a greater sense of comfort with our long-distance relationship and counted down what was only a matter of weeks.

My time on *Lizard Island* coincided with the global financial crisis. By early 2009, the resort was increasingly feeling the economic impact of the GFC but continued to operate reasonably successfully, although not without implementing some hefty discounts to its rates. Nevertheless, occupancies were lower than usual.

Then came the week from hell.

There had been sightings reported by some staff of two crocodiles who appeared to have taken up residence on rocks

## Lizard Island

at the opposite side of the island. The presence of saltwater crocodiles that far out on the reef was unheard of at *Lizard*. I immediately called the Crocodile Management Unit in Cairns and requested them to investigate the sightings and remove the creatures from our shores. I was asked how big the crocodiles were and said they were probably less than two meters... Which was a mistake, because the response I received from the unit was, *'Ah, nothing to worry about there with crocs that small'*.

I protested at length, stating that their mere presence could be catastrophic for our business, let alone the repercussions should an attack take place. The person I spoke to was adamant they did not have the resources to send someone over to capture crocodiles which were non-threatening. The advice given was, *'Just keep an eye on them.'*

*'What, until they get big enough to actually attack someone?!'* I asked, with more than a hint of sarcasm.

I was told that the crocodiles would probably leave our waters of their own accord and return to more regular habitat closer to the mainland.

Okay... So now, 'keeping an eye on crocodiles' was added to my list of duties in this 'idyllic' place! I asked Trystan, the Boats Manager, to keep a *very close eye* on the activities of our resident crocs and to alert me immediately should they show any inclination to be travelling to the resort side of the island.

A few weeks elapsed without incident, but we had not seen the last of them. However, before that, another crisis was brewing with some concerning weather conditions heading our way.

Cyclone season in North Queensland typically runs from November to April each year. In early March, we began to receive warnings of severe storm activity in our area. During guest drinks one evening, Trystan called me aside to advise that the situation was worsening, and it was possible that a cyclone would hit *Lizard* in the next 24 hours.

As such, he needed to move the resort's million-dollar deep sea fishing vessel to safe harbour in Cooktown. He planned to leave first thing the following morning with a few of his strongest crewmen. I gave him the go ahead to proceed.

The Rooms Division Manager, Chief Engineer and Nurse were all off island on holiday at that time which meant with Trystan also leaving, I did not have a strong group on site to deal with the looming crisis. And I had never dealt with anything like it before.

Earlier in the season, I made a thorough review and updated the cyclone procedure documentation in place.

I had worked through the updated procedures several times with the team, including comprehensive checklists of who was responsible for what in a cyclone situation, and felt relatively comfortable that we had everything covered.

That evening, I communicated with all department heads to begin their lockdown preparations and with guests to say that we would plan for as many to leave the following day *if* flights were still operating from the mainland – otherwise they would need to prepare for lockdown too.

Overnight, the weather became more extreme. Winds increased significantly, and the sea turned into what looked like a giant washing machine with waves crashing on to our normally tranquil beach.

## Lizard Island

At first light, Trystan and his boys set off on *Fascination* (the yacht) for what was going to be a very choppy passage to Cooktown. Trystan assured me he could handle it but needed to move quickly before the full brunt of the storm hit later in the day.

Most guests had opted to stay on the island, assuming that flights would not be operating and regardless, did not want to risk a turbulent crossing to Cairns in a small plane. I was in touch with *Voyages* head office in Sydney and was told that at this stage, the morning flight was still on schedule and would only be cancelled should winds exceed 40 knots per hour.

This meant more guests would be arriving which made me very nervous. However, it was not my call to cancel flights, I just had to get on with handling the situation onsite.

The villas were built to be cyclone-proof but the main lodge which housed the restaurant and kitchen were not. While I co-ordinated staff with supplies to occupy vacant villas and appropriate supervisors to oversee guests with emergency provisions, everyone else was busy preparing themselves and their departments for the impending Category 4 storm, which was on track to cross *Lizard* in the late afternoon.

Every boat had to be removed from the water and roped down as securely as possible on the beach, every piece of furniture in the lodge moved out, bottles and glasses in the bar wrapped in plastic, boxed and placed in villas, pool furniture submerged in the swimming pool to prevent it blowing around, and so it went on.

The Executive Chef had worked tirelessly overnight to prepare countless eskies with food, water, emergency lights, etc., and label each one with which villa the supplies were to be delivered to. I was extremely thankful to have all those detailed and updated procedures we had worked on earlier in the season at my fingertips!

Mid-morning, I called the managers at the Research Station to check in with them. They had been on the island for almost 20 years and dealt with several emergencies during that time, so I was keen to ask their opinion on how serious conditions might become. They didn't think *Lizard* was going to take a direct hit but were still preparing for lockdown of the station and its staff. Their words gave me some comfort.

The morning flight left Cairns as scheduled and was due to land on *Lizard* at around 12 noon. It just so happens that this was the Labour Day holiday in Victoria and was the weekend that Sam and his parents had booked to visit me on my 'tropical paradise'. All were on that Friday morning flight, along with some other guests and a few staff members. I watched the plane complete its descent over the water towards the island's runway and it was being heavily buffeted by strong cross winds. On board, conditions must have been terrifying.

After two aborted landings, the pilot radioed us in the control room at the property to say he would have to return to Cairns: *'Copy that pilot. We do have clear sky over the runway right now, would you be prepared to give it one more attempt?'*

He was prepared to. And successfully landed the small plane amid much cheering, but some very ashen faces of the passengers who disembarked.

I did not have much time to welcome Sam's family as I had other guests to brief and assure that the situation was under control but yes, the resort was in lockdown mode, however it was hoped this would only be a temporary measure.

By early afternoon, the wind had continued to increase in power and rain was coming down in sheets. I made one last round of the property in a buggy to check that everything had been made as secure as possible and visited guests in their villas to let them know who would be supporting them through a full lockdown and what to expect (but in reality, I had no idea of 'what to expect').

All employees were either in the staff dining room with some of the management team or with me and a smaller group in the back office of the lodge with radio communication between the two areas. Everyone had been briefed of their lockdown location and would make their way to it immediately when the time came. In the office, we were closely tracking the path of the cyclone.

Time ticked over very slowly, but gradually the situation began to look less dire. The afternoon flight landed with a small group of similarly shaken guests as in the morning. Part of lockdown procedure is, for obvious reasons, a total ban on alcohol consumption. As such, a mocktail had been prepared as a welcome drink for arrivals, instead of the usual champagne.

One guest took a look at the offering and said, 'After what I've just been through on that flight, you've gotta be kidding me... I need a large scotch!'

And he seemed to be in no mood for negotiating on his demand. We served his drink and then, naturally, everyone else wanted alcohol too. I acquiesced as there had been a definite easing in the weather with some patches of blue sky appearing and even a watery sun trying to break through. I was reasonably sure we were not heading for full lockdown so asked staff to gradually start a clean-up and ready their departments to resume business as usual that evening.

The Research Station management had been correct – once again, *Lizard Island* had been by-passed and spared the full force of a cyclone.

Trystan called to say that he was safely in Cooktown which I was relieved to hear. He reported that the weather had also begun to settle on the mainland and if it continued to improve, he would return with *Fascination* the following day.

After a brief pre-dinner drink with guests and, now that the cyclone had passed and the weather forecast for the rest of the weekend was excellent, we could all see the amusing side of the day's events. I staggered home exhausted thinking that I'd need to take Sam's family for dinner in the restaurant, which was definitely not something I felt like doing as I hadn't stopped for close to 24 hours.

Instead, I was delighted to find a delicious barbeque ready to serve at my place. Sam's mother could tell the enormous pressure I had been under all day and decided that a casual dinner at home was going to be the way to go. I blessed her thoughtfulness.

Sure enough, Saturday morning presented with the most beautiful weather you could wish for, which was an unbelievable transformation from the previous day. Everyone was in great spirits with the resort resuming normal operations. But the weekend had yet more twists and turns to come.

Sunday was set to be the highlight of Sam's family visit as we had booked *Fascination* for a private excursion to the outer reef to go fishing and snorkelling. Sam and I had made this outing when he came up in December and it was the best part of what had been overall a dismal visit, as he had spent a good deal of time alone while I was working. We were looking forward to repeating the magical day with his family.

## Lizard Island

Before leaving, I popped down to the office to remind staff I was going to be offsite and check all was in order before I headed out.

When I arrived, the Front Office Supervisor was having an intense conversation with someone on the radio. That someone was a medic with the Flying Doctors who were enroute to *Lizard*. One of the receptionists proceeded to fill me in on what was happening.

A dive boat, several of which frequented our waters and anchored close to the island to conduct snorkelling expeditions, was experiencing a medical emergency involving one of their clients and had contacted the resort for assistance knowing that we had a full-time nurse onsite. The dive boat team were currently at a nearby beach conducting CPR on their client, who appeared to have suffered a heart attack in the water while snorkelling.

Our nurse was off island and the Restaurant Manager was the back-up in this situation since she held senior first aid certification. She was already on her way to the beach with several from the water sports department who were also trained to perform CPR. The crew from the dive boat realised that the situation was serious from the outset and hence their call to the Flying Doctors for professional medical support, but the plane was a good hour away. When there was still no response from the patient after 45 minutes of resuscitation attempts, the doctors said there was nothing they would be able to do by the time they reached the island and that our next step should be to contact the coroner in Cairns.

Sam was by now at the office wondering what was causing my delay, so I had to quickly fill him in on what was unfolding.

*'Maybe we can still go out on the boat later?'* he asked, but the look on my face indicated not. Neither *Fascination* nor I were going anywhere that day!

The next few hours were an avalanche of activity with calls to my manager in Cairns for advice on what the procedures from here needed to be. Technically, it was not our problem as the resort was not directly accountable for what happened and had merely provided assistance. The deceased person was not our guest, and we had not been involved in any way with events leading up to the emergency. However, there was a body on the island close to our resort which had to be dealt with, and we had the resources available to provide further support.

Everyone involved in the attempted resuscitation was quite traumatised and our HR Manager was in touch with counselling services on the mainland arranging passage to *Lizard* as quickly as possible. They arrived within a few hours, as did the coroner and representatives from Workplace Health and Safety.

Trystan, thank goodness he was back on the island, was relatively calm and in control even though he had been involved in providing CPR to the man who died. The body needed to be moved from the beach to somewhere cool… But where? Trystan suggested the walk-in fridge of the staff bar which I agreed was the best option. He handled the transportation quickly and efficiently.

We set up a villa to be used as an interview room for the coroner and Workplace Health and Safety, and another for the counsellors to provide staff support. The management of the dive boat were in the process of conducting calls to next-of-kin for the deceased man who had been holidaying alone.

The resort was not busy and there were only 10 villas occupied, so around 20 guests. I spoke to them all individually to provide an update of what had happened and the reason for all the unusual activity around the resort. Most were understanding of the disruption, but a few were feeling very short-changed from their expensive stay on *Lizard Island* particularly considering the recent cyclone event which had also affected normal services. I tried to be as sympathetic as I could but my stress levels by this stage were through the roof. And about to explode…

I was in the process of briefing the coroner and about to drive him down to examine the body in the refrigerator of the staff bar, when I felt a tug on my arm to attract my attention, *'Yes, what is it?'* I said as patiently as I could, but it probably came over as quite snappy.

*'Wendy, er…someone has just reported the sighting of a crocodile near our beach.'*

I swear I'm not making this up! I asked Trystan to deal with the coroner while I had a receptionist print 'BEACH CLOSED' signs and went off to speak with guests yet again about the latest debacle.

*'So, now we can't even use the beach?'* some of the more disgruntled clients exclaimed.

*'I would definitely advise against it,'* was about as much of a reply as I could muster.

By early evening, all the investigations had been completed. The dive boat crew were back on their vessel, the coroner and workplace health and safety team had flown off the island with the deceased man and I had spoken to as many of the staff who had been involved in the incident as I could. The Restaurant Manager was understandably distraught being the senior first-aider in attendance at the emergency. I assured her she had done an outstanding job, as had everyone, to take whatever time she needed over the next few days and ensure to conduct a full de-brief with the available counsellors.

It was another late-night home for me and another makeshift but delicious dinner from Sam's mother. I was so disappointed about how the weekend events had impacted the family's visit, but they were totally understanding saying they'd still had a good time, which I doubted.

I thought that Sam could have been more supportive as the crises unfolded, but perhaps I was expecting too much from him. The family returned to Melbourne the following day leaving me with the crocodile situation still to resolve.

First thing Monday morning, I received a call from the Crocodile Management Unit in Cairns. The local media had reported a fatality on *Lizard Island* which the representative wanted to find out more about.

'How much do you know?' I asked.

'Not a great deal. It wasn't the crocodiles, was it?'

'Well, no. It seems that the tourist suffered a heart attack while snorkelling during the morning and couldn't be revived. However, a crocodile was sighted close to the resort late yesterday and our beach has been closed since then,' I replied.

'Okay Wendy, we'll have someone out to you today who will hopefully capture the crocodiles.'

'That would be appreciated, as soon as you can please.'

## Lizard Island

Mike was the epitome of a crocodile hunter – a tall, muscular fellow with shoulder length hair and a laid back but very competent manner. He spoke to all the staff who had actually seen the crocodiles over the last few weeks and was able to piece together a fair account of their movements. Mike planned to go out that night to track down the animals. Trystan and a couple of other alpha males on his team wanted to accompany the croc hunter which I reluctantly agreed to.

The next morning, Mike said he had good and bad news. The good news was that a crocodile had been captured but it was not the one seen in our video footage – it had completely different markings. That would concur with the original report of two having been sighted basking on rocks at the opposite side of the island.

'So, back out tonight I suppose?'

Correct.

The star of the video was indeed picked up that night and the following morning was in 'safe keeping' in the water sports storeroom together with, but not too close to, the animal that had been captured previously. I was most impressed with Mike's efficient handling of the situation. He assured me that he'd had a good look around the whole island and was confident there were no other crocodiles out there. He was most surprised about the two's presence on *Lizard* in the first place as he'd never heard of 'salties' that far out on the reef before.

A cargo flight was arriving on the island that morning and the plan was for Mike to accompany the two crocodiles on the return empty leg to Cairns. The animals were boxed up in secure containers which Mike had brought over, ready for the flight. I accompanied him to the airfield ready for loading, but the two large boxes would not fit on the plane as well as Mike. The pilot refused to fly without Mike being there for safekeeping of the cargo, which I completely understood.

There was a suggestion that one of the crocs be left on the island and Mike would return the following day to collect it.

*'No way,'* I said, *'You either stay here to keep guard over both of them until we can secure a larger plane, or you have to find a way of getting them and you on this plane.'*

He could see I was deadly serious. After briefly weighing up options, Mike took the boxes off the plane, opened them up and proceeded to put both crocs in *one* box. That certainly caused a fair amount of thrashing around to occur, as you can probably imagine! But Mike expertly sealed up the animals again and reloaded them on to the plane.

*'You're a star Mike, thanks so much,'* I said. Honestly, I could have kissed this giant of a man but gave him a big hug instead. He left with an, *'I'll be off then, bye.'*

I let out an enormous sigh of relief as the plane headed into the sky and away from the island.

That night, I slept soundly for the first time in almost a week. It had been exactly seven days since preparations for the cyclone began, which we were thankful to have escaped the full force of, only to have been immediately faced with an equally tumultuous series of events and emergencies. I had survived it all, but only just.

Fortunately, the holiday to *El Questro* with Sam was just a few weeks away. After four days there, we were travelling back to Melbourne together for a longer break during which time we would be attending the wedding of one of Sam's friends for whom he was the best man.

The stay at *El Questro Homestead* was fantastic, and we had a great time. I felt though that Sam was somewhat distant with me which I put down to the fact that, just before our holiday, I had agreed with my boss to stay on at *Lizard Island* for another two months, since the sale of the property was drawing close to completion. The mood between Sam and I had been a tad cool since the family visit to *Lizard* in March and back in Melbourne we also struggled to connect.

I had a fair bit of time for soul searching during the wedding we attended while Sam was busy with his duties as best man. When I looked around at so many of his friends who had already tied the knot or were in the process of doing so, some even starting families, I pondered the fact that I'd just turned 52 years old, and Sam was not yet 30. I knew it was time to let him move on and enjoy a more regular life with a partner his own age. And I had an inkling that he felt likewise.

During my time in Melbourne, we decided to go our separate ways. It was a difficult and emotional decision for both of us.

I returned to *Lizard Island* and stayed until September, almost a year to the day from when I started. The Restaurant Manager decided she needed a change after the trauma of the medical emergency and was offered an internal transfer with *Voyages* which she was very happy about.

Her successor came from the fine dining restaurant on *Hamilton Island*, and he brought with him a few members of his team. Nikita, the new Restaurant Manager, was a first-class operator and a lovely person. He was the reason I extended my tenure for longer than planned. The crew Nikita brought with him were all extremely competent food and beverage professionals, and quickly turned *Lizard's* restaurant around.

A few weeks later when the new brigade had settled in, I was in the restaurant one evening still working there as usual. Nikita approached me with one of his typical broad smiles and said, *'Wendy we love having you in the restaurant, but I think we can take it from here now. Why don't you have an early night?'*

And that's exactly what I did! From thereon, the only time I needed to spend in the restaurant was to play host to guests rather than serving them, which was far more enjoyable than directing the service periods day after day. Sometimes, I would surprise myself (not to mention many others) and venture down to the staff bar for a spot of socialising before heading home at the end of the day.

On the weekend before I left *Lizard Island*, I made a final tour of the resort and was very satisfied with how it presented and the many improvements we had implemented since I'd started there. It had been an incredibly turbulent 12 months both professionally and personally, but I probably felt prouder of my achievements there, in a relatively short space of time, than anywhere else I had worked. It was such a challenging period when for the most part I felt intensely uncomfortable in the environment, yet it won me over in the end and now whenever I look back, I feel so privileged to have spent time in such a beautiful part of the world.

Next stop was Melbourne and an empty house at Richardson Street. There would be no Jake and Benson who had moved in with me all those years ago, and now no Sam either as he'd moved out to live in his own place a few weeks before my return.

## Lizard Island

The difficult adjustment to a life that had changed so completely in just 18 months continued. And the dark moods that had once again descended during my time on *Lizard Island* were set to intensify and become more frequent in the months ahead.

I had little time to myself on Lizard Island so would always try to get up early before there were any guests or staff around and take a big walk around the island or work-out in the gym. I liked to listen to some lively music which would prepare my headspace for the inevitable challenges ahead of another day in 'paradise'.

My go-to band was INXS and their iconic album 'Kick' released in 1987, which still sounded great over 20 years later. There were many hits from this album but it's the opening lyrics from one song which instantly transport me back to those solitary early mornings on Lizard Island.

Playlist Track 19: 'Mystify'

At the end of a long day, it was something gentler that I tuned into. A song which I discovered during this chapter of my life was from the 2004 re-release of 'Rumours' by Fleetwood Mac. The album was an expanded version of their 1977 mega-hit with additions of several outtakes from the original recording sessions, including this one featuring the unmistakable vocals of Stevie Nicks. My playlist track is actually the 2013 remastered version which I later came to prefer.

Playlist Track 20: 'Planets of the Universe — Demo'

# 17

## Siem Reap, Cambodia

Okay, so luxury island retreat is ticked off my bucket list of hotel management experiences with no desire to go there again. So, let's move on to somewhere else on the list.

Over the years, I had contemplated a stint in Asia. During the latter stages of my term on *Lizard*, I put out a few feelers in that direction. A recruitment consultant in London, with whom I had worked previously, had two opportunities on her books for General Manager positions she thought might be of interest – one in Luang Prabang, Laos and the other in Siem Reap, Cambodia. I had spent a very pleasant few days in Luang Prabang a few years earlier, so was familiar with that location. I had not previously visited Cambodia.

Within a few weeks of returning to Melbourne, interviews had been organised by the recruiter and I was soon jetting off to Bangkok from where I would make the necessary connections. Both hotels had the same owner who I met in Laos, and he briefed me about the role in each property.

*Hotel de la Paix* in Siem Reap had been operating successfully for several years. The property in Luang Prabang was still in the process of being converted to a luxury hotel after being the town's former prison. Hence, the opportunity in Laos was a pre-opening position which I knew would bring its own set of unique challenges.

In Cambodia, I met with the Managing Director of a Bangkok based company which managed *Hotel de la Paix*. Eric is a well-respected veteran of luxury hotel management and was with *Four Seasons* in Asia for many years. He is a delightful man, and we chatted for a long time. By the end of our conversation, I was keen to work with Eric and an inspection of the stunning property consolidated my interest in the role. I was also taken on a tour of Siem Reap.

The area is much more than just a base for discovering Angkor Wat, although the ancient temples are what attract millions of tourists each year from all over the world. By 2009, Siem Reap had several five-star hotels, trendy bars and cafes, fine dining restaurants and an array of fascinating shops selling locally made products. It is also the base for many non-governmental organisations (NGOs) run largely by ex-pats from western countries involved in programmes to assist with socioeconomic improvement.

All in all, it was a lively little place which I felt had more to offer in terms of lifestyle than Luang Prabang. This was an important consideration for me given the isolation I'd felt on *Lizard Island*. The owner of the hotels also thought I would be better suited to Siem Reap and his feedback to Eric sealed the deal for my position in Cambodia.

Back in Melbourne, I was once again packing and this time preparing for an international move. Reluctantly, it was time to

## Siem Reap, Cambodia

relinquish the lease on Richardson Street and dispose of many belongings to reduce storage costs. While looking forward to my upcoming venture overseas, the process of packing up the house and parting with so many possessions, which should have symbolised closure on the past few years, instead left me feeling quite distressed.

The situation was further complicated by a resumption of relations with Sam. This began with occasional catch ups but had progressed into conversations about getting back together and him joining me in Cambodia once I established myself there. But as the time for my departure approached, I realised this outcome was unlikely to eventuate. Once again, we found ourselves engaged in painful 'what if' scenarios and emotional farewells.

I managed to keep myself focused on the amount of organisation that moving country entails despite suffering frequent bouts of anxiety and depression. I hoped that a fresh start with a new job in a completely different environment would be the fix I needed for my see-sawing mental health.

Arriving at *Hotel de la Paix*, I immersed myself in the new role where there was plenty to take in. I had a good management team who were most welcoming which made the settling in period relatively easy. The staff to guest ratios were much higher than in Australia, but most employees needed more direction than I was accustomed to.

The aftermath of the atrocities inflicted by the Khmer Rouge 30 years earlier, when virtually a whole generation of the country's inhabitants had been wiped out, meant that most people still lived in poverty which accounted for the many NGOs who operated throughout Cambodia.

Employment in a luxury hotel was highly sought after, being a secure and more pleasant environment in which to work than many other options available to young people with limited education and resources.

Once employed, individuals were fearful of losing their job should they make any mistakes. I encouraged everyone to be more confident in their abilities, assuring them that no one would be fired for making a wrong decision or by speaking up. Still, it was a long road to build their confidence. In common with the population in general, the staff were young and lived in awe of authority.

*Hotel de la Paix* was actively involved in several community projects, the primary one being a sewing centre which supported disadvantaged females. The women arrived at the centre through a variety of circumstances such as homelessness, domestic abuse or injuries sustained in workplaces where they had completed heavy manual labour. They were provided with accommodation and meals, as well as remuneration for making clothes and household items which were sold in the on-site shop.

The hotel promoted tours of the centre to guests, as well as to other charitable organisations in Siem Reap. Guests would usually make donations and purchase goods which were available for sale, thereby providing much needed financial assistance. The hotel also directly donated money, food and clothing on a regular basis as further support.

When I started, Eric informed me that one of the community projects he wanted to see completed was a major renovation of the sewing centre. The previous manager had been trying to formalise plans but without success for one reason or another. I was keen to get things moving as quickly as possible and started to spend some time with the women at the centre each week.

## Siem Reap, Cambodia

After everyone became accustomed to seeing me around and asking questions about what was needed, they began to relax and communicate more freely about how the facility should be redesigned. I soon had a good idea of what was required.

Another community support programme was the display of paintings and sculptures from local artists, and every few months *Hotel de la Paix* would host a party in its Arts Lounge to launch new exhibits. These parties were very popular and attracted hundreds of the town's ex-pats.

At one of these events, I met Sabine. She was a French national working locally as an architect, and I spoke to her about the renovation of the sewing centre. Sabine was keen to help on a pro-bono basis as she was familiar with the facility and the benefits it provided. She subsequently presented her proposal which the women at the centre reviewed and a few refinements were implemented. I asked Sabine if she could have someone build a model of the new sewing centre for the hotel to display alongside flyers on the works being proposed and the need for funding.

The model looked fantastic as a centrepiece of the Arts Lounge. Our guest relations department had frequent interaction with hotel clients as they were the liaison point to book restaurants, flights, tours and so on. I requested staff to show the model to as many guests as possible and brief them on the project including the need to raise funds.

The reality was that we required a fair amount of money to get the work started. The plan was to raise half the funds from guest donations and the balance would be financed by the hotel. Our guest relations team did a remarkable job in creating awareness for the project and before long, donations were flowing in from guests who had visited the sewing centre and wanted to help with the renovation. The amount of donations being received previously was minimal, but soon we were pulling in close to $5,000 each month. It didn't take too long to reach our target.

During one of my regular catch ups with Eric, he congratulated me on the display of the sewing centre in the Arts Lounge and asked how it was all going. I told him that the design plans had been finalised and a builder had been recommended so we were ready and keen to commence before the approaching monsoon season.

*'But, what about the funds to finance it?'* he asked, and looked totally astonished when I told him we had raised the required amount and, along with the hotel's contribution, were good to go. Eric was elated and couldn't believe how we'd managed to get this project off the ground so quickly.

A few months later, I was invited to attend a conference at the *Four Seasons* in Singapore to make a presentation on *Hotel de la Paix's* charitable works, along with other organisations in the region who ran successful and sustainable community projects. It was a very satisfying part of my role to be involved with the many charities supported by the hotel.

There was an initiative revived at the hotel which also gave me a great deal of satisfaction. The Human Resources Manager wanted to resurrect a meeting between the GM and staff which had previously taken place on a regular basis but had fallen by the wayside some time before I came onboard.

The meeting involved having one employee from each department, who was not a manager or supervisor, to meet with the GM as a group for an afternoon tea and discuss any concerns within their department or more general issues associated with their employment. I thought this sounded like a great idea and scheduled the meeting to recommence each month.

Refreshments were made available, which was always a big draw card to ensure attendance, and I encouraged representatives from each area of the property to raise anything at all they wished to discuss with me.

At first, there wasn't much participation as employees were afraid to speak up for fear of retribution. However, once the staff realised that their suggestions were being taken seriously and actioned wherever possible, there were an increasing number of matters raised.

We were able to roll out many simple improvements which directly affected staff such as the quality of their meals, onsite parking facilities, uniform availability and improved air conditioning in some of the more oppressive areas of the workplace such as the laundry.

The meetings were fun, productive and often ran well over their time. Representatives reported back to their departments and provided feedback on the meetings which helped breakdown the 'us and them' mentality. I became aware that, as I toured the hotel, staff began to approach me with more confidence by making eye contact with a big smile instead of bowing their heads.

One day, while chatting with a few female staff, they told me how proud they were to work at *Hotel de la Paix* because it was the only luxury property in Siem Reap with a female GM and how inspired that made them feel to pursue a career in hospitality. I was very touched.

It seems that Cambodia had been a good move for me, right? Yes and no.

I was generally enjoying my new role and the team I was working with. I also found Siem Reap fascinating and met interesting people with whom I was able to have a reasonable social life. But when home alone, depression was a frequent companion.

I knew I had been using alcohol and sleeping pills for some time to self-medicate and numb the sense of hopelessness that would often envelope me.

After a particularly miserable Christmas Day and copious amounts of self-medication which led me to seriously question the point of my life, I decided it was time to seek professional help. I made contact with an Australian psychologist in Phnom Penh and flew to the capital on Sundays, my only day off.

The therapist was a woman from Melbourne who was having a spell in Cambodia with her husband and young family. At our first meeting, I told her how my life felt like it had been unravelling over the last couple of years; about losing my boys, taking redundancy after 10 years in a position that I really enjoyed, how an exciting future with that company had been snatched away and finally of my relationship breakdown.

The therapist assured me that any one of the changes I described was cause for some degree of anxiety and depression, and to have had so many upheavals in such a short space of time would have significantly escalated the triggers for a more serious breakdown.

It was helpful for me to hear this as I'd never really linked the various events and had compartmentalised each at the time when it occurred. In some ways, I found it reassuring to know that I was in fact suffering with many layers of grief which, by this stage, needed to be dealt with collectively rather than individually.

There was also another 'small' matter which I threw into the mix and that was my increasing sense of panic related to ageing. I was 52 at the time and informed the psychologist that I had absolutely no desire to grow old. She asked me how old I thought was 'old' and wasn't sure how to answer but when pushed to put a number on it, I said that anything over 60 would probably be too much for me. Oh dear!

After around five sessions, I was definitely feeling better but didn't have any deep engagement with the doctor nor did I think we were advancing beyond progress made in the first couple of visits, so I decided to discontinue the therapy. In the meantime, a friend from Australia came to visit, and I found spending time with someone who knew me well and with whom I could speak openly helped enormously.

Hannah had just broken up with her boyfriend and was feeling somewhat conflicted about the future too. We had some great chats and plenty of laughs which I'm sure helped us both. When Hannah said she would like to stay on in Cambodia longer term, I persuaded Eric to employ her on a contract basis to overhaul the hotel's marketing material. Hannah's background in writing and editing meant she had the ideal skills for what was needed, and Eric agreed it would be a good idea to hire her.

Around nine months into my tenure at *Hotel de la Paix*, I conducted a sales trip to London and followed that with a holiday at home with my mother. While I regularly spoke to her on the phone, I hadn't visited for two years. Mum was now close to 80 years old, but she was still active and healthy. She had only recently given up riding her bicycle every day! I always asked whether she needed any financial assistance and lately she had more frequently accepted my offers of help. This was perfectly understandable as the relatively small amount of money my father had left all those years ago would have been all but exhausted by then and Mum only had her pension to rely on.

She owned the house and lived quite simply so her expenses were not excessive. Overall, I thought my mother was in good shape and I had no real concerns about her when we spent a few weeks together in 2010.

The time away allowed me to reflect on the changes I'd been through in the last few years. One of the insights was that it seemed like I'd been running away from everyone and everything that might remind me of the earlier happy years in Melbourne – initially to a remote island in Australia and now to an even more distant location in Cambodia.

While there was much to like about Siem Reap, it is a very different culture and a transitory environment where ex-pats came and went regularly. Not to mention the climate! In April, which is usually the hottest month of the year before the monsoon rains come, it hit 48 degrees Celsius with over 90% humidity… Most unpleasant.

That was extreme even for Cambodia, but the country is incredibly hot and sticky virtually all year-round. When I first arrived, I would go for an early morning walk, but that soon became unbearable. In addition to the heat, locals burned their rubbish including large amounts of plastic making the air acrid from all the smoke. I soon gave up the morning walk and retreated to air-conditioned comfort in the hotel gym for my exercise. However, I didn't find it particularly pleasant to live my life in air-conditioning.

## Siem Reap, Cambodia

By the time I returned to Cambodia after the sales trip and holiday, I had made up my mind to resign from *Hotel de la Paix* and return to Australia. I realised it was there that I really wanted to live and, with no partner or close family, be amongst a network of friends who I could rely on for support.

I spoke to Eric about my decision, and he completely understood my reasons. He recognised that 'Cambodia is not Asia for beginners', which was my situation. A starting point of somewhere like Bangkok or Singapore is usually regarded a more suitable environment for Westerners as an introduction to Asian culture before potentially tackling less developed locations in the region, like Cambodia.

Hannah was coming to the end of her contract with the hotel at the same time as my planned departure date and we decided to travel together before heading back to Australia. We began by volunteering at a *Save the Bears* sanctuary in rural Cambodia which was quite an experience.

From there, we utilised many of my hotel contacts to stay in some beautiful properties in Vietnam and Laos and ended the vacation at Raffles in Singapore which was a memorable end to our holiday.

In November 2010, I was on my way back to Melbourne once more, this time with nowhere to live and no job in the pipeline. I tried to push these concerns aside but, as might be expected, they were a source of some anxiety. However, I was by then comfortable financially so decided to take a few months break from work, recharge fully and use the time to make the right decision about 'what' and 'where to' next.

Note: *Hotel de la Paix* in Siem Reap is now a *Park Hyatt* and the property in Laos which I also originally interviewed for is the *Sofitel Luang Prabang*. Both hotels continue to enjoy excellent reputations.

Even so, I was sorry when I heard that neither were still independently operated, instead had become part of large chains. Sadly, that's how many great boutique hotels often wind up and, in my opinion, lose some of their unique personality in the process.

# 18

## Resurrection in Sydney

As 2011 dawned, the only decision made about my future was that I wanted to live in either Melbourne (preferably) or Sydney. After two relatively short tenures on both *Lizard Island* and in Cambodia, I wanted to take my time, be sure about the next role and hopefully settle into a career progressing move which would set me up for several years to come.

I also needed to find somewhere to live as moving around, which I'd been doing for a few months since returning to Melbourne, was unsettling. I was about to rent something on a short-term basis, which is an expensive option, when a friend offered me to stay in his rather grand apartment at the city end of St Kilda Road, which was only used a few days each week as mostly he lived at his (also rather grand) house in Lorne.

*'Stay as long as you like, I'm hardly ever there,'* he said. It was so kind of him, and I felt very fortunate to have my own space in somewhere so comfortable and convenient.

A few job prospects began to trickle through but nothing that I felt particularly enthused about. On one of my trips to Sydney, I met Marc with whom I used to work at *Hotel Lindrum*. He had transferred to Sydney a couple of years earlier for a position with a small boutique hotel company called *8Hotels*.

I had crossed paths with *8Hotels* and its charismatic founder, Paul Fischmann, in 2004 when *Cbus Property* had expressed some initial interest to purchase the *Kirketon Hotel* in Darlinghurst. Paul acquired that property at the time.

Over dinner with Marc, he informed me that *8Hotels* was expanding and he thought there may be an opening for someone with my background and experience. He provided me with an introduction to the company's Head of Human Resources.

Rowena and I bonded immediately over shared values, particularly the importance of building a strong organisational culture, providing teams with regular training and development opportunities and the provision of exceptional guest service. I met Paul later and while he wanted a business with the qualities I'd discussed with Rowena, he was also focused on the bottom line and keen to bring someone on board who had proven experience in driving revenue and controlling expenses. Both Paul and Rowena thought I would be a good fit for *8Hotels*.

However, Paul was concerned that his business at that stage had an insufficient number of hotels to justify a new Head of Operations, along with the salary expectations of such a role. I was sure from the outset that this was the right move for me and during weeks of ongoing conversations, Paul and I managed to keep the negotiations open.

Finally, about two months later and with a few compromises on both sides, the contract was agreed on and signed off, with a start date in early May.

Due to the protracted nature of the recruitment process with *8Hotels*, I had convinced myself that a successful outcome would probably not eventuate. During this time, there had been other offers of employment which I turned down as I didn't want to run a small individual property nor to work for a large company with multiple layers of management. None of the offers were for a group role which I was hoping to secure with *8Hotels*. I began to worry about my situation should Paul ultimately decide against recruiting anyone for a new senior position, or that he might meet someone else who was more suitable to join his growing business.

As a result, I began to catastrophise about my future which led to further bouts of extreme anxiety. This time around though, I had friends close by and one of them in particular was a tremendous support to me.

I met Larissa and John through Sam, and after our break-up, I thought that might be the end of my friendship with them, but they clearly did not want this to be the case and the three of us became close. I spoke to Larissa regularly from Cambodia and was most surprised when, just before I returned to Melbourne, she asked me to be bridesmaid at her marriage to John.

I was honoured but had my concerns, *'Larissa, it's so sweet of you to ask me, but honestly don't you think I'm way too old to be a bridesmaid?!'*

She would not hear a word of it, and eventually I gave in.

In the lead up to the wedding I had a serious meltdown and Larissa was the one person with whom I felt I could share the extent of my mental health problems. She managed to get an appointment with an excellent psychologist in the city and accompanied me at the early sessions with Rachel to ensure I was being completely open.

Larissa knew me well enough to suspect that until now, therapists were only receiving a somewhat sanitised version of what I wanted them to hear rather than the whole truth. And she was right, that's exactly what I'd been doing in the past. With Larissa in the room though, I had to be honest about answering questions such as whether I had ever thought about suicide and, if so, did I consider how I might take my life. My response was 'yes' to both questions.

Rachel was naturally alarmed to hear this and considered possibly sectioning me (being placed in hospital under the Mental Health Act). I managed to assure her my rock bottom had passed and promised to stick this time with the professional treatment I so obviously needed. I also now had the help of a good friend close by, a factor which had often been missing when 'the black dog' previously showed up in my life.

In common with previous therapists, Rachel was concerned about the amount of change I had been through in recent years without a support structure in place from family or friends. My upcoming move to Sydney represented yet another big upheaval where I would once again be in a position of having no one nearby to whom I could turn for assistance.

We set to work on improving my balance and stability as much as possible in the short time available before my relocation. I was given lots of homework which kept me focused on my mental health during the days when Rachel was not available for a consultation and dear Larissa checked in on me twice a day for several weeks. Everything we were doing to improve my wellbeing resulted in the fog slowly but surely clearing. I started to feel much sharper and calmer.

While we concentrated on my more recent history, Rachel said my childhood should be revisited too. This ongoing therapy though would have to wait until after I settled in Sydney with referral to a psychologist there.

My healing continued when I moved to Sydney. While I still suffered some anxiety and depression, it began to feel more 'normal' and something I could manage without falling into the depths of despair. Since that time in early 2011, my suicidal ideations have never again resurfaced. I count myself extremely fortunate.

The move turned out to be a very positive life changer for me. I found a lovely apartment in Potts Point, a buzzy inner-city suburb of Sydney, which was also the location of *8Hotels* office and meant I had the convenience of being able to walk to work each day. My new role was everything I had hoped it would be. The business was on the cusp of substantial growth, I was working with a dynamic group of colleagues and had a smart, supportive boss.

When I joined the company, there were just seven hotels for which I had operational responsibility. They were located in Sydney, Melbourne and Canberra, with the General Managers of each property reporting to me. *8Hotels* also had marketing agreements in place with another hotel in Brisbane, some villas in Bali and apartments in Paris. It was quite an eclectic mix!

In the first six months, expansion was rapid and *8Hotels* acquired another five properties which I oversaw the transition and ongoing management of – one in Sydney, one in regional Victoria, another in Brisbane and two in Perth. Needless to say, I was constantly travelling.

In addition to this, we embarked on two other major projects; the company moved its headquarters to a larger space in Surry Hills and we also rolled out a new property management system across all hotels in the group.

During this relatively short period of time, when our feet hardly touched the ground, Paul and I recalled with some amusement his concerns during the recruitment process when he thought the business was too small to support my role.

By the end of 2011, we were operating 12 properties in five states and the rate of acquisitions slowed down after this initial period. Even so, by 2013, *8Hotels* had expanded to 15 hotels, adding two more in Sydney and another in Melbourne, which meant that the company then operated over 1,000 rooms and had 250 staff under its management. These were busy, yet exciting times.

A year after joining *8Hotels*, it was Easter and I had a few days off, during which I reflected on how much my life had improved during the last 12 months. It can be hard for people to understand how anyone would willingly choose to spend major holidays alone. However, after such a busy period of work and travel, it was a welcome relief to be enjoying four days on my own with no fixed plans. There were no appointments to keep or agendas to meet, and I could do exactly what I wanted in my own time.

I felt happy and privileged to enjoy that sort of freedom. Solitude is not necessarily loneliness; it can be rich and joyous. As I grow older, I am increasingly aware of the importance to have quiet times alone to recharge my energy. During that Easter break, it felt so good to be in the moment and realise that I had pretty much all I needed. And all that I needed was simpler than I perhaps once thought.

## Resurrection in Sydney

The small but comfortable apartment where I lived had a balcony where I could sit, enjoy a glass of wine and appreciate my surroundings. I overlooked beautiful gardens which provided a sense of calm and balance to a busy life in the middle of a large city.

I had a job which gave me a great deal of satisfaction, utilising my expertise from a lifetime of managing hotels but without the 24/7 on call commitment of being the General Manager of an individual property. Journeying frequently to different parts of Australia, I loved spending time with younger managers to guide and support them. Virtually everyone in the company was at least 20 years younger than me and I had wondered how my age might be accepted when I took on the role. But everything was working out.

In turn, I enjoyed learning from the team who kept me on my toes with different ways of doing things and breaking some of my 'old school' habits. I'm sure it kept me young at heart too.

By this stage, I had been single for a few years and was increasingly content with that situation. Friends would often ask whether I felt lonely not being in a relationship. And occasionally I did, but equally had no desire to relinquish my freedom. I had enjoyed several very fulfilling relationships but, at 55, I felt like this was 'my' time.

Therapy had continued during that first year in Sydney with someone I was referred to by Rachel. After a few months, when my childhood trauma, teenage eating disorder and self-harm as a student were all revisited, I felt stronger mentally than I had in years.

The psychologist thought we only needed to meet intermittently in future when he mentioned we should explore my sense of shame – if I was open to it. This had never been previously mentioned, just something the therapist had picked up on during our many conversations but sensed I had not been ready to confront. When he said this, almost casually in passing, I felt as though a sharp blow had been struck deeply to my core.

Finally, the layers with which I had been protecting myself were unwrapped and someone had gotten to the heart of the matter. But he was right about me not being ready. And in the sessions that followed I would carefully side-step any approach to the subject of shame. Then I began to make fewer appointments and eventually stopped seeing the psychologist altogether.

It was in some ways quite a relief to stop dragging up the past and fully embrace the life I was enjoying in the present. Perhaps I should have persevered longer, but I'd had enough of talking about myself.

There were many highlights during my time at *8Hotels* and one of the most rewarding periods was undoubtedly the opening of a new Sydney property in 2013. The building was heritage listed and located in Pyrmont, next door to Darling Harbour. It was originally constructed in 1888 (which became the name of the hotel) as a wool store. Paul had been working with the owners for some time on this project and was excited about adding it to the *8Hotels* collection as the company's flagship property. He was intimately involved in all aspects of the hotel's design for which he has a very keen eye.

The team was handpicked from the best of the best at our other hotels in combination with recruitment of external talent. In addition, the head office management team, as the opening date approached, dedicated their time exclusively to the *1888* launch. The marketing team worked closely with a public relations consultant and came up with some novel campaigns.

## *Resurrection in Sydney*

Some readers may remember the international online coverage about the world's first Instagram hotel back in 2013. That was *1888*.

The sales team leveraged their existing relationships within the corporate and leisure markets to drive business into *1888* from the day it opened. Rowena delivered innovative and comprehensive pre-opening training programmes to ensure the team were ready to hit the ground running.

The GM had been working at *8Hotels* for several years and had performed outstandingly as manager of the *Kirketon* prior to his appointment for *1888*. I worked closely with him on the operational requirements for opening which encompassed all aspects of setting up Front Office, Food and Beverage, Housekeeping and Maintenance.

There was also the usual array of compliancy processes which had to be documented and rolled out, such as Fire and Emergency Plans, Food Safety programmes, Workplace Health and Safety policies and establishment of maintenance schedules for the plant and equipment in a new hotel. All rooms and public area spaces, every piece of furniture and each appliances had to be checked several times with any defects noted and made good by the builders prior to opening.

Even though I had already worked on a number of pre-openings over the years and had my processes and timelines finely tuned by this stage, there is *always* more work than you anticipate, and it *always* takes longer to get things done than you predict, and this *always* results in long hours of work with little time off. It was, however, one of the easier openings in my experience, largely due to the quality, focus and diligence of a very capable and committed team.

The collective efforts were rewarded and *1888* was an immediate success. The property enjoyed phenomenal occupancy rates from day one, which is virtually unheard of for a new hotel, particularly when not part of a recognisable chain. One might have expected service levels to have been compromised during this unexpected explosion of opening activity, but that did not happen, and the extensive staff training paid off supremely as did the unwavering hands-on support of the front-line team by the GM and his 2IC.

Positive reviews on *TripAdvisor* – *the* most influential guest feedback platform of that time – came thick and fast. Within eight weeks of opening, *1888* was the number one rated hotel in the whole of Sydney. This was way beyond our most optimistic predictions for the new property. It was a credit to all involved.

But success can sometimes have a downside... And in the case of *1888*, there were soon approaches from larger hotel companies who wanted to acquire this highly regarded property and make it part of their own portfolio.

The sale of *1888* in 2014 to *Ovolo Hotels* coincided with a change in direction for *8Hotels*, with Paul deciding to considerably pare back his business.

Before these changes eventuated though, there was a family crisis unfolding back in the UK which required my attention.

*Two songs resonate from this period in my life when the tide finally turned for me after a few extremely challenging years.*

*The first is from Robbie Williams who has been very open regarding his earlier battles with mental* health. The sentiments expressed in this highly successful single connected with me during the times when I too was lost in a cycle of depression.

Playlist Track 21: 'Feel'

The second reminds me of winning my fight with 'the black dog' — not really what the song is about, but it's how I relate to the lyrics. It's an adapted version (which I prefer) of an earlier song, released by Anastacia in 2015.

Playlist Track 22: 'Army of Me'

# 19

## *Did You Know?*

---

As my mother grew older, I had been visiting her regularly for several years. In 2011, she celebrated her 80$^{th}$ birthday and the following year my aunt remarried. Janet's wedding was the last time when the family were all together for a joyous occasion.

When I saw my mother in 2013, she was considerably frailer than when I'd seen her the year prior, although still in quite good health. I started to think about returning to the UK on a permanent basis so that I could spend more time with Mum during the latter stages of her life. It would be a big move after calling Australia home for over 20 years and I pondered the idea for several months before taking any action.

When the changes at *8Hotels* were announced and it appeared likely that I may be looking for a new job in the foreseeable future, I thought it might be time to re-establish contact with the recruitment agent in London and ask her to keep me informed of any employment opportunities which might facilitate my return.

We had a long telephone conversation in early February 2014 regarding what I was looking for in a new role and my preferred locations in the UK. The agent said there were a couple of positions on her books that might be of interest which she would follow up and get back to me about.

The following day, a call came through from my mother's number with brother-in-law, Ron, on the line. My alarm bells immediately sounded. He informed me that Mum was very unwell and needed to go into hospital, but she was refusing to do so before speaking with me.

Apparently, she had been sleeping in an armchair for several weeks due to breathing difficulties if she lay down, and by now her legs were heavily swollen due to fluid retention as well as having a lung problem which was placing considerable pressure on her heart. I had a quick word with my sister Sally and then she put Mum on the phone. I tearfully pleaded with her, and she agreed on being admitted to hospital.

I spoke to her doctor each day who told me that mother's condition was serious but not life threatening and that she should recover fully once the build-up of fluid was brought under control. I received a call from Janet a few days later who said that Mum was sitting up in bed and would like to talk to me. I was relieved to hear her sounding so bright, unlike during our previous conversation before she went to hospital – in fact my mother said she hadn't felt this well in a long time.

I shared with her my plans for a permanent return to the UK, as I thought this would further boost her spirits. We continued to chat daily and within a week or so, the hospital was planning for her to be discharged. I had been looking at available flights to the UK since receiving the news of Mum's health problems but placed these on hold since she seemed to be recovering well and getting back to her normal self.

After returning home, however, she went downhill rapidly. Sally, Ron and their daughter were taking turns to look after Mum but, as the days passed, their concerns mounted. My mother was becoming increasingly vague, having difficulty communicating and could not perform simple tasks for herself. She was readmitted to hospital.

I was in Canberra at the time, overseeing the *8Hotels* property there which was being transitioned to new owners within the coming months. Paul was aware of my mother's predicament and totally supportive of me leaving to be with her whenever I needed to go. I let him know the time had come, and that I had booked a flight to London the following day.

I stopped by the *8Hotels* office, on my way to Sydney airport, where I received a call from my sister. She told me that our mother had died a short while ago. I was shocked but not totally surprised. I had been praying that Mum would hold on at least until I could see her and was angry at myself for not having travelled home sooner.

It was another long flight to the UK, reminiscent of 20 years ago when I had made the same miserable journey after my father suddenly passed away. I arrived in London late on Saturday night and stayed with Colleen, before making the final leg of my journey by train the following morning. My sister and brother-in-law picked me up from the station and that's when, after the details pertaining to Mum's final hours were related to me, the conversation took an extraordinary shift.

*'Did you know that Mum sold the house?'* Sally queried. Sorry… What?! How could she have; she was still living there. Yes, I was told, but it appeared that our mother no longer owned her home as it had been mortgaged back to a lender. My sister had apparently been to the house and collected boxes of documentation which she couldn't make much sense of.

At the time, it didn't cross my mind to wonder why Sally had already gone through Mum's property so thoroughly; it had been barely 48 hours since she'd passed away. I later realised that my sister possibly had some inkling regarding the declining state of our mother's financial affairs which was why she had collected the paperwork so quickly. I knew that I needed to look at everything myself and try to piece together the puzzle.

We went back to my sister's house where I was staggered by the volume of material she had gathered. My organisational skills immediately kicked in. I set about reviewing every piece of correspondence and sorting it into chronological order by institution involved. There were loan documents, credit card bills, unpaid utility invoices, bailiff's notices and incredibly, the purchase of an apartment.

*'Oh, didn't you know about that?'* asked Sally. *'It was for Mathew.'*

I did *not* know about this.

Mathew is Sally's son. Another shock wave hit me.

Over time, several loans had been taken out by my mother using her house as collateral. There was the name and signature of a female who witnessed some of these documents which I queried with my sister.

*'Do you know who this is?'* I asked.

## Did You Know?

'Ah, I think that might have been Mathew's girlfriend at the time,' Sally said. Hmmm…

My aunt had offered for me to stay with her and after several hours of compiling all the material into some kind of order, I informed Sally and Ron that I was exhausted but would take the paperwork to Janet's and continue working through it. My aunt had prepared a meal for me and afterwards I felt sufficiently refreshed to start again, despite her protestations that I needed to sleep. She went to bed while I got back to work, making notes on the most pertinent information and then adding timelines of when loans were raised and with which institution. I continued throughout the night.

By morning, I was severely jet-lagged after travelling through multiple time zones with little sleep for several days. When Janet came to see me, I said, *'Oh my god, not only was Mum penniless when she died but she has left significant debts. I don't understand how this has happened, considering she led such a simple lifestyle.'*

*'No way'*, Janet replied, *'I can't believe it. Are you sure? It makes no sense. But let's talk about it later, you really do need to get some rest.'*

I fell into bed and slept for eight hours straight.

The whole sorry saga began after Dad passed away. Mum owned the house and had been left a tidy sum which, together with my father's and her own pension, should have been sufficient to support her. Mum didn't smoke, drink, run a car or take holidays. Her biggest extravagance was visiting the hairdresser on Saturday for a shampoo and set! She used some of the money Dad left to have renovations completed on the house and I could see a few relatively large amounts being drawn down from her bank account to fund these works.

Thankfully, Mum had kept everything, so I had her bank accounts as well as other documents dating back to the mid-1990s, which proved to be very helpful. These records enabled me to trace the movement of her money in a far more detailed way than I would otherwise have been able to do. Even so, I was never really able to get to the bottom of the mystery of how her finances deteriorated so significantly in a relatively short space of time. I have my own ideas about what may have happened but will keep those opinions to myself.

My mother always had a soft spot for her grandson, one of the reasons for which became clearer when I was later informed about another 'little gem' from the family history, and I can understand why she wanted to help him by purchasing an apartment as he needed somewhere to live. When Mathew later moved out Mum sold the property, but by then the market was in recession and, taking into account expenses related to buying and selling, she wound up significantly out of pocket which had a detrimental impact on her financial position. I had no idea about any of this at the time.

I briefed Janet on the numerous documents which demonstrated an escalation in my mother's monetary woes, with her situation quickly spiralling from bad to worse. There were loans on top of loans and, when repayments could not be maintained, threatening letters were sent by several creditors.

The most recent bank statement revealed that when Mum's pension was deposited, all the funds were immediately being transferred to the most persistent of the institutions who were owed money, which left her with nothing to live on.

## Did You Know?

Her house was also about to be repossessed, and she would have been homeless.

It was little wonder that in recent times, Mum had been asking me to send money or pay some of her larger bills on a more regular basis. Janet informed me that both she and Mel had also been approached periodically by their older sister for financial assistance.

By the time of her hospitalisation, my mother would have known it was time to reveal the whole catastrophe to the one person who had the means to resolve it – me. But I'm also aware of how reluctant she would have been to do so thinking that, while I lived in Australia, she might still find it relatively easy to hide the reality of her situation from me.

The announcement of my plans to return and live in the UK, however, was going to make it far more difficult to conceal her predicament. Janet then relayed something I found very disturbing. Apparently, when Mum had first heard my news she was excited but soon after, possibly having reflected on the likelihood of me finding out about the state of her affairs should I be living close by, seemed far more down-beat and said to Janet, *'Tell Wendy not to come home, I'm perfectly fine and don't want her to give up a good life in Australia for me.'*

I know that my mother would have done *anything* to save herself the embarrassment of telling me the mess she was in and equally would have been in complete anguish about having to virtually ruin me financially in order to save herself. I firmly believe that it was the stress of my imminent return, and all its implications, that put the additional pressure on Mum's already weakened heart which led to her sudden passing.

One of the saddest letters I found amongst all the paperwork was from a widow's society my mother had written to, asking for their help. It was totally heartbreaking to think of what Mum must have been going through for years, and particularly in the last few months of her life.

And what did it say about me as a daughter, that she felt unable to share her problems? I was beside myself with the grief of it all. A part of that grief was regret surrounding my unexpressed love to Mum before she died. I know I'll never really get over it. But there was yet more to come!

It was another *'Did you know?'* question, this time from Janet. She asked me whether I was aware that Mum had given birth to a son before she married. No, I was not! Crikey, so now, after everything else I've discovered in recent days, I also learn about a half-brother floating around somewhere in the world for over 60 years! Janet did not know the identity of the father and by then, anyone who might have been able to shed light on it had passed away.

Mum had been sent away to another town in the later stages of her pregnancy and gave the child up for adoption soon after its birth.

My Uncle Mel, who was around four years old at the time, vaguely remembers his older sister moving away for a few months and it was only much later that he discovered the reason.

When they were both older, Mum provided a few details to Mel about what happened; her son was adopted by a couple, and she had some limited knowledge about him until the family moved overseas. And that was the last she heard. Once again, I felt great sorrow for the tragic circumstances that had befallen Mum and about which she felt unable to confide in me.

## Did You Know?

The loss of her son must have had a tremendous impact on my mother who was only a teenager at the time, and I think it helps explain the strong attachment she had to any males in our family – her (half) brother Mel, son-in-law Ron and grandson Mathew.

It was also at this time when Janet told me the truth about Mel's father and that he was *not* Charlie's son, which is what I had grown up believing. The twists and turns within my family just kept on coming!

I was lucky to have a very good friend to whom I could turn for personal support as well as professional advice. I would always meet Deborah, my best mate from school, for a meal or drinks whenever I returned home on visits. Deborah had been a partner in a local law firm for many years and I called her as soon as I had a clearer picture of my mother's affairs. She had known my mother well and was extremely sorry to hear of her passing.

When I told Deborah of Mum's financial situation, she was horrified and asked me to visit her office as soon as I felt up to it. A few days later, I was taking her through the details and although she was concerned by the amount of debt my mother had incurred, she could see that the extent and organisation of all the paperwork would give her a head start in opening the file. It would be over four years before that file could be closed.

I had hoped to speak at Mum's funeral but knew, as the time approached, I would not be able to do so as my emotions were way too ragged. It was a beautiful, clear and sunny spring day to say goodbye to my dear but secretive and troubled mother. Bless her.

The previous weeks had really shaken me, and I needed time alone to process everything that had happened. I looked at the mass of paperwork I'd taken back to Sydney and kept going through it all in utter disbelief.

An email with a job opportunity from the recruitment agent in London had in the meantime arrived. I let her know that my mother had suddenly and unexpectedly died, therefore, I no longer had any real motivation to move back to the UK. Isn't it astonishing how the universe can conspire to hijack your plans?

I was obviously never meant to leave Australia.

Deborah and I were in regular contact during the months that followed. She advised that there was no alternative but to sell the house which would hopefully pay off the main secured creditors. There would still be a large amount of money owed to other institutions, so she set about trying to have those debts written off as well as shielding me, being my mother's official next-of-kin, from possible litigation.

The house eventually sold but unfortunately not for anything like the amount we hoped, however it had been on the market for 18 months without any offers, so it was let go. Sally said from the outset, she didn't want to get involved with the legalities of handling Mum's estate, so I had power of attorney to make decisions. Therefore, while Sally was disgruntled with the house sale, she was not able to contest it. As the months dragged on, Deborah managed to persuade some of the creditors to write off my mother's debts, but others were being more stubborn and wanted settlement.

Naturally, there were fees being generated by Deborah for the work she was doing. I had paid an initial amount for her to get started and a few months later asked for an estimate of what the eventual costs might be. I telephoned Sally to inform her there were charges Deborah would need to pass on, and could she possibly assist in any way with some of these expenses? I received her response via email.

## Did You Know?

I sat on my anger for a couple days before responding to Sally and let her know how disappointed I was to hear that she expected me to foot the whole bill for a legal debacle left to us by our mother. I informed my sister that I would take care of everything but that I wished never to speak with or hear from her again. And, after a lifetime of suffering Sally's prickly temperament, I was actually relieved that this was the end of our relationship. I let Deborah know of the correspondence with Sally and she was equally appalled but told me not to worry as she would keep the billing to a minimum.

Time rolled on and finally Deborah had agreements from the last of the creditors. This meant the file which had been opened several years ago could be closed and I would receive the long-awaited invoice. I took a deep breath before I opened the attachment on Deborah's email, read through all the work that had been completed to finalise my mother's affairs and reached the end which stated, *'Balance Due'* with the word *'NIL'.*

I questioned this with Deborah, but she assured me it was correct and that she had made her decision after my sister declined to help. Deborah said something like, *'I simply could not allow you to be responsible for everything. None of it was your fault. That's what friends are for.'*

I realised in that moment how some friendships in life are priceless, and how right I'd been about the decency of the girl I met and became 'besties' with when we were just 12 years old.

This has been the most distressing chapter of my life to write about, but at the same time, it feels like a huge weight has been lifted by recording many of the events as they played out. There are more details that I could have included but it would have been just too overwhelming to have done so. However, I have added a few post-script notes, as follows.

## Aunt Janet's Marriage

After 30 years of marriage, Janet and her first husband divorced quite acrimoniously. She met her second husband a few years later and both were in their early 60s when they decided in the summer of 2012 to tie the knot and throw quite an extravagant wedding, which most of the immediate family attended. It was a lovely day.

Mel looked very handsome and gave Janet away. Mum was radiant in her new outfit we'd bought for the occasion and even my sister and I got along well. We were all delighted to see Janet so happy.

Sadly, my aunt's new life was cut tragically short a few years later. She was diagnosed with leukemia in 2018 and died less than 12 months later, just before her 70th birthday. Janet had been like a sister, then later a mother, and her death hit me hard. She remains sorely missed.

## The Search for My Half-Brother

Since finding out about the son my mother gave up for adoption, I've had bouts of interest in finding him, alternating with no desire at all to do so. I've spent hours on the UK Registry of Births, Marriages and Deaths piecing together details of my extended family covered in earlier chapters.

I have also trawled through birth registrations in the whole of the east of England during the late 1940s to try and track down my half-brother, with only my mother's maiden name with which to filter that search.

I thought I had been successful when I found a baby born in June 1949 (my mother would have been 17 then, so the timing seemed about right), in Cambridge (far enough for Mum to have been sent away from the prying eyes of neighbours), the father was listed as 'unknown' and the child's name was the one I knew my mother had given him.

It looked like a perfect match, but to be sure, I needed a copy of the birth certificate with the mother's full name and address, so I had a copy sent to me in Australia. As I opened the envelope, I was so excited, but alas, the name and address did not belong to my mother. It was another dead end.

## A Psychic Reading

A few years ago, I visited a spiritual guide. Even though I had not mentioned it, the guide picked up strongly on my mother's passing. I made notes as he spoke.

*'Your Mum had a difficult transition from life and there were things she never told you because of shame and embarrassment and did not want to burden you with her worries. She had a very good heart and it was her desire to do the right thing, even though others may have done the wrong thing… But still, she always wanted to keep her door open…'*

Phew, that took a while to process!

I include a song for this chapter which was one of my mother's favourites and was played at her funeral. It always makes me think of her.

Play List Track 23: 'Islands in the Stream' by Dolly Parton and Kenny Rogers

# 20

## Checking Out

After the personal upheavals of early 2014, I was looking forward to immersing myself in the routine and distraction of work. I headed to Canberra to complete the transition of *Diamant Hotel* to the *Peppers Group* which settled mid-year.

Afterwards, I was glad to be living full-time in my Sydney apartment again. Despite Paul's intention to sell more of the *8Hotels* collection, I opted to stay put and prioritise stability by remaining in a familiar role and see how the work situation progressed over time.

By 2015, more of the company's properties were on the market for sale. The downsized head office team was now working once again out of the smaller Potts Point office where I had been based originally.

During the years when our collection of properties had been continually growing, we had been able to attract many talented individuals who were keen to work in such a stimulating and exciting environment. However, the mood now was far more subdued and several of the team began to move on in search of new opportunities.

I had also been involved in some tentative discussions with other operators. A position arose that I was keen to pursue and quite quickly an offer was on the table. I spoke to Paul who was concerned about losing a key member of his management team and I thought he was trying to protect his own interests when he urged me to turn down the position saying, *'The company isn't right for you, the building you'll be based in has serious issues and, on top of that, dealing with the demands of the commercial tenants who lease space in the property adds yet another layer of complexity.'*

But I thought I knew best, so decided to move on anyway. I had spent five very rewarding years with *8Hotels* and felt the time had come for something new.

Well, as usual, Paul turned out to be right! I realised on day one in my new role that I'd probably made a mistake. By the end of the first week, I was reasonably sure of this and after the first month was ready to walk away. However, in case I might be jumping the gun, I stuck it out for a bit longer. During that time, when the situation on the work front failed to show any signs of improvement, I decided a long vacation was needed and started to plan a holiday to Europe and the UK.

I gave three months' notice when I resigned and wasn't worried should the company have asked me to leave immediately but, surprisingly, they did not. Six months of my life I'll never get back… Haha.

## Checking Out

What made this position, above all others in my extensive work history, so intolerable? There were numerous factors which I will not go into other than by commenting that I'm no stranger to hard work and long hours but struggled to keep up with the demands placed upon me.

I was immensely relieved on the day I left and couldn't wait to get away for my holiday in Europe. I flew to Majorca, where I checked into a rather lovely spa hotel and spent a few days there chilling out and recovering from my previous work environment with treatments, delicious food and lazing by the pool. I then had some time in the capital, Palma, before heading over to the Spanish mainland to meet my old friend Colleen in Cordoba.

We had a fantastic time in that beautiful historic town and afterwards travelled down to San Pedro to visit Heidi which, as always, was great fun. I went on to Lisbon, another captivating city which I really enjoyed exploring. Next stop was the Algarve in southern Portugal, after which I headed to Israel for a week. I wanted to explore somewhere a bit different on this trip, and Israel proved to be a fascinating country.

My final destination was London where I caught up with Colleen again, as I had done many times over countless years of journeying back and forth to Australia. I made a side-trip to my old hometown which felt bitter-sweet. It was sobering to re-visit Fortune Street and check-out my old family home which brought back many difficult memories, as well as the property where my friend and her mother had been murdered over 50 years ago.

But there were good times, too, and it was lovely to catch up with my Aunt Janet and Uncle Mel as well as childhood friends, Deborah and Anne. I have not returned to the UK since that last time in 2016.

The holiday was exactly what I needed. I had been away for eight weeks, felt fully refreshed and was ready for another new challenge as GM for a pre-opening, a position which had been offered to me before going overseas. Sadly, this role didn't really work out either. I loved the stylish property, and its owners were excellent to work for, but my interactions with some other key figures within the organisation were less harmonious.

A few months later, I was having one of my regular catch ups with Paul Fischmann who by then had divested most of the original *8Hotels* collection. He was in the process of opening two interesting new properties, both of which had been potential development opportunities when I'd worked for Paul previously.

One was the *Felix* at Sydney Airport which was in full pre-opening mode and under management contract to *8Hotels*. The other was *Little Albion* in Surry Hills, a beautiful heritage building that Paul owned, which was undergoing a complete restoration to create a modern hotel. I expressed an interest in opening this property and Paul was very keen to have me onboard working with him again. There were no drawn-out negotiations this time around and we signed off on the deal within a few days.

I returned to *8Hotels* at the beginning of 2018 and commenced by assisting with opening the *Felix*. The General Manager had been with the company for several years and I had previously worked with Simon who I really liked, as well as having enormous respect for as an operator, so I knew we would have an enjoyable time together getting the *Felix* up and running. And that we did.

A few months later, I relocated to concentrate on opening *Little Albion* which had been beset by ongoing delays. It was, however, worth the wait. Paul had done an amazing job on this property which had become his baby – although an expensive addition to the family!

I knew how stressed Paul was due to the cost blowout on this project, but at the same time, he wanted it 'right'. As usual, the opening meant hard work and long hours, but I was prepared to do both for this special property and its owner. Described as, *'Delightfully intimate, devastatingly gorgeous, genuinely original and refreshingly unpretentious,'* Little Albion boasted all this and more.

But guess what? Shortly after *Little Albion* successfully opened to great acclaim, Paul informed me he had accepted a good offer to sell the property. Aaagh! The company who purchased *Little Albion* had been making some serious inroads into ownership and operation of luxury hotels around Australia for a few years. By the end of 2018, I was no longer working with Paul, but for the new owners, *Crystalbrook*.

By then, I'd had enough of being the GM of a small property and desired a more senior position which would fully utilise my skills and knowledge. Several months later, a very interesting opportunity presented which took me back to Melbourne. It turned out to be a fantastic role, working with a superb team and an inspirational leader, which I thoroughly enjoyed. However, …

During the two years of my tenure, COVID arrived and Melbourne endured some of the longest and strictest lockdowns of any city in the world. In 2021, with yet another lockdown of the city being announced, I came to the realisation that the end of my career was rapidly approaching. I looked back on the last four years which had included opening two hotels back-to-back and moving interstate to take on a senior role for a business in which I was required to learn many new skills, followed by the demands of managing that business through COVID.

All of which was weighing on me both physically and mentally. I was turning 64 years of age and had to accept that the time had finally come to check-out. I retired in July 2021.

It had been 46 years since embarking on my career in hospitality, which began in 1975 behind the bar at a charming hotel in the English countryside. After the early days in food and beverage, I moved on to front office and sales, then was promoted to oversee rooms division departments. I became a General Manager and later was responsible for multiple properties in senior executive roles.

It had been quite the voyage through five countries and three states within Australia. I had remarkable memories from along the way, and a few disappointments – but hey, that's life! There were many wonderful people I'd met, some of whom remain cherished friends to this day.

My identity had always been largely defined by the success I achieved at work, and it was only natural to wonder how I might handle a future without the structure of a job to keep me grounded. I had plans, but first needed to take a break and relax!

*Throughout my career, I have been fortunate to have worked with and for many smart, supportive and motivating people, mostly men. In my last hoorah, though, I encountered one or two who were less than inspiring and to whom I often responded in a very direct manner, which led to me being labelled as 'difficult'.*

# Checking Out

During lockdown in 2020, 'folklore' was released by Taylor Swift and this Grammy-award-winning album became a firm favourite of mine. There is one song with its (somewhat) restrained feminist message that I now listen to with a wry smile as it reminds me of two hotel roles briefly mentioned in this chapter and the 'stings' I apparently inflicted during my time in both!

Playlist Track 24: 'mad woman'

# Afterword

Well, there need not have been any concerns about dealing with potential fall-out at the end my career and how to cope with such a momentous change. From the moment I stopped working, I haven't looked back.

The plan had been to return to my house I bought some years ago on the Sunshine Coast in Queensland, which I'd thought at the time might eventually be a retirement home. However, in July 2021, Queensland's borders were closed due to COVID. So, I was stuck in Melbourne.

This was not such a bad thing initially, as Ken was returning from Vanuatu where he'd been living for several years and had a gorgeous little dog, Max, he wanted to bring back to Australia. I advised him to have Max sent to me in Melbourne, which is the only place where animals can be quarantined in this country, as soon as possible, so that I could mind the little fellow before sending him to the Gold Coast when Ken arrived home.

Max and I spent two very pleasant months together keeping each other company during lockdown. In the meantime, there was still no sign of Queensland opening and it began to feel like I was treading water in Melbourne, becoming increasingly frustrated about not being able to move forward with my life.

I decided to start heading north at least as far as New South Wales, as the borders there were open subject to inter-state travellers having been vaccinated. My friend, Brenda, had been living in the Southern Highlands for several years after she returned from Vietnam, and I'd often visited her when I lived in Sydney.

She was happy to have some company after being in lockdown herself for several months. I always really liked Bowral and had considered it as a potential location for retirement, so it made sense to check out the area properly before I made a firm decision about Queensland. The day after I dispatched Max on a flight to the Gold Coast, I was flying to Sydney, on my way to stay with Brenda.

At Christmas, the borders to Queensland opened and I went there on holiday for a few weeks. I decided then that the Sunshine State was not where I wanted to live, its sub-tropical climate being just one of the reasons it didn't appeal as a long-term base. I drove back to Bowral and as soon as I returned, it immediately felt right for me to settle in this charming regional town. Within a couple of months, I'd bought a property here after selling the house in Queensland.

Since then, I've been busy making improvements to my little cottage, which has been such a joy after living in rented accommodation for so many years. I work one or two days a week, helping with the various needs of a regular group of elderly clients and people with disabilities, which is genuinely rewarding.

My new and less demanding lifestyle has given me time to write this memoir. That spiritual guide I mentioned in an earlier

## Afterword

chapter said to me, *'The next 20 years may be the happiest and most fulfilling that you experience.'*

Thus far, he's been absolutely right with that prediction. I couldn't be happier.

This writing journey has caused me to think about the many different pathways available in a lifetime and how we weigh them up. How, when we're young, we tend to regard our lives stretching into a far distant future, and it doesn't matter if a few mistakes are made along the way. Which it doesn't, so long as we learn from those mistakes. But, if poor choices are continually made, all too soon, the years have passed and we may find ourselves in old age, looking back with some regret on the decisions taken and the opportunities which were discarded.

I've also pondered the ways in which we might find the right balance in life and how to counter negative emotions with positivity. I believe that our energy comes from what we read, listen to, watch and where we focus our time and attention. And, very importantly, with whom we spend our time.

To end my story, I would like to pass on a few personal and professional life lessons. There are some we might be mindful of in both areas of life:

> *Should you encounter issues of **trust** with someone, walk away as quickly as possible.*

> ***Be careful by who you surround yourself with.*** *If most of your friends and acquaintances lead chaotic and troubled lives, it's likely that's how you may wind up too*

because their habits rub off and become normalised. As a leader, it's equally important to surround yourself with the right people.

**Treat everyone with common decency and respect** regardless of their status in life or position in an organisation.

**Speak less and listen more,** whether it's with friends or colleagues. Just do it!

As a leader, a few of the truths I've learned along the way are:

**Hire the best you can find** and build a team with multiple complementary skills. And never let your ego get in the way of recruiting someone stronger than yourself.

**Do as I do.** Should team members fail to see you walking the talk, leading by example and giving your best effort day-in and day-out, they won't give theirs either.

**Be less concerned about being liked than being productive.** This doesn't mean to actively engage in being disliked, on the contrary, you want your best people to feel motivated working with you, which they won't if they dislike you. But beware of taking the path of least resistance with non-performers, because if you are seen to tolerate mediocrity, then that's what you will get.

**See failures as your own and success as belonging to the team.** When I hear someone talking about the

## Afterword

accomplishments of their business in the first person, 'I did this, I did that,' my alarm bells immediately ring. It's likely that, when something goes wrong, they might say, 'Unfortunately, **we** failed to anticipate...' A true leader will frame success in terms of 'we' and negative outcomes by taking personal accountability.

I conclude with sharing some insights that have served me well personally, particularly as a woman:

**The importance of a good education** and to continue the quest for learning throughout life. You can choose to read great books, listen to informative podcasts or watch movies that make you think, as well as inspire and entertain you.

**Don't always adhere to what societal expectations dictate.** The traditional expectations of women, prescribed largely by men for over 2,000 years, have been seriously challenged in more recent times. My parent's generation was probably the last in which women were generally expected to become wives and mothers above any other aspirations. I understand that this is still a natural course of events for many women who desire and gain immense satisfaction from raising a family. Others successfully combine a career with motherhood.

It's probably not surprising, given my background, that I saw having children as entrapment into domesticity and chose to remain childless. It was the right decision for me, and I have no regrets. I've therefore led quite a different existence as a female but one which has still been incredibly fulfilling and continues to evolve in ways I could not have imagined. So, question societal expectations and, if those 'norms' don't rock your boat, consider alternatives. It will obviously help if you can support yourself financially and, in this respect, unless you're born into wealth, acquiring a decent education will definitely be an advantage. As will be the ability to get your head around the next point.

**Be comfortable in your own company** and nurture the things you value and want to spend time involved with.

**Call out double standards.** I was reminded of this while reading an article (Eleanor Danenberg, ABC Entertainment, 'Something's Gotta Give at 20 years old', April 2024) marking the anniversary of that great movie, which caused quite a stir when it was released in 2004. A pivotal scene involves discussion of the 63-year-old character played by Jack Nicholson being **celebrated** for his endless relationships with much younger women and having never married. It's argued that a woman in a similar situation would most likely be regarded **very** differently. And that was 20 years ago. Has anything really changed since then? The double standard of gender is still far too prevalent in many situations, and it needs to be called out more often.

During the Introduction and in a later chapter, I wrote that even quite recently I was not prepared to confront my issues around shame. Feelings of inferiority have been a constant shadow since childhood and caused me to always limit my expectations on the level of success I could achieve in life.

## Afterword

I've also heard that shame is a great driver of perfectionism. This made me smile. Ah, so now I understand why I studied so hard, worked so tirelessly and judged myself so harshly for any perceived shortcomings. Better late than never, I suppose, to shed the ideal that I, or anyone else, should or can be perfect.

However, having been completely candid during the writing of this memoir, I feel like there's nothing to hide from anyone anymore. It has been liberating to belatedly confront, in my own words, the demon that's been on my back for way too long.

Looking back, I've dealt with a few ordeals along the way, but have been blessed with so much good fortune too. One of the greatest gifts has undoubtedly been my ongoing physical health, which I try never to take for granted. I have also benefitted from numerous educational and career opportunities presented over the years.

I count myself lucky for having good friends and to have known the enjoyment of several rewarding personal relationships with kind and decent men. And not forgetting the unconditional love for and from my boys, Jake and Benson.

It's a life, I think, that's been fully and well lived.

There have been several accomplishments in my 67 years, but the one I'm most satisfied with is probably the one you're reading right now.

I'm thrilled to have completed my story which has demanded such discipline to stick with over the last two years. There *will* be a book that I've created sitting on a shelf at home which is all mine. Even if no one else reads it.

And finally… I feel so very proud of myself.

The last song is another composition from the poet of our times, Taylor Swift, featured on her 2020 album 'evermore'. There are two reasons why I chose this track to wrap up. Firstly, it's a reminder that we never really lose those we have truly loved, they are always with us.

Secondly, in this chapter which includes a few of the things I've learnt along the way, the lyrics provide some sage advice for us all as we journey through life.

Playlist Track 25: 'marjorie'

# Acknowledgements

I have to start with a massive thanks to my good friend Larissa Leone for her unwavering support not only through some very tough times in my life but also for encouragement to write this memoir – particularly when I was a few chapters in and thinking of giving up. You, my dear, have been instrumental in keeping both me and this project alive.

To Chris Fitzpatrick and Paul Fischmann who ploughed through the *very lengthy* early drafts of my manuscript and provided such positive feedback, while urging me to *'just keep going'*.

Chris, you know how much I enjoyed working with and the great respect I had for your husband Kevin. Thank you for closely reviewing 'his' chapters and gently pointing out a couple of my errors.

Paul, what can I say other than heartfelt thanks for my life-changing appointment to *8Hotels* and trusting me with your businesses, not once but twice. And what a ride we had!

To other dear friends who also endured the rough early edits of my manuscript – Brenda Jarvis, Connie Beltran, Simon Farr,

*Life for Rent*

Tish Black and Keith Patrick. Thank you all so much for your time and kind words.

Hats off to Ken, my ex-husband, for approving the chapter 'Shattered Dreams', even though it was not *quite* how he remembered it... Haha! And of course, for the love and friendship we have shared for almost 40 years, not to mention tracking down two very special puppies for my birthday in 1993. You have been and will remain a very cherished part of my life.

Thanks to everyone on the 48 Hour publishing team, especially Vivienne Mason the Publications Manager, Alex Floyd-Douglass my Editor and Nik Boskovski the Book Cover Designer. Your patience throughout the copious number of changes I've requested has been greatly appreciated, and your guidance indispensable, making this journey somewhat easier to negotiate than I imagined. Though, I must admit, it is not something to be embarked on by the faint-hearted!

To illustrator Alexandra Nea, who was an obvious choice for me after the many incredible marketing images she produced for the last hotel I opened and managed – *Little Albion* in Surry Hills, Sydney. Thank you for the beautiful image created for my book cover which I like to refer to as, *'Jake and Benson at Little Albion'*. I love your work!

To Alyce Evans at *Studio Legal*, thank you for helping me manage the legalities of my story. Your thorough yet sensitive delivery of concerns raised in the manuscript, together with recommended changes, has been invaluable.

Sincere thanks to those other close friends who have played an important role in my life story and also agreed to be named in this book – Anne, Colleen and Heidi. We go back a long way!

## Acknowledgements

A very special mention to Deborah, my best friend from high school who, many years later, so generously navigated me through the chaos left behind by my darling but troubled mother. Words cannot express my gratitude and how privileged I feel to have you as a friend.

To my Uncle Mel who recently turned 80, and incredibly is the only family I have left. I'm delighted that you wanted 'the honour' of being named in my book even though I suggested a pseudonym. It's been many years since I've seen you and your lovely wife Jos, but hopefully we will catch up again before too long. Until then, I will continue to treasure the times we get to chat on the telephone.

And finally, thank you to my boys, Benson and Jake, for bringing such joy to my life.

# About the Author

Wendy Morris was born and raised in a small country town of rural England.

At primary school, she passed her 11-plus exam to attend the town's prestigious grammar school which empowered its pupils for tertiary study. Wendy went on to complete a degree course in Hotel Management at the *University of Surrey*.

Her career spanned 46 years, initially in the UK and later South Africa, Greece, Cambodia and Australia. She acquired a wealth of experience in opening and managing luxury hotels in London, Cape Town, Siem Reap, Melbourne and Sydney, as well as remote locations in the Greek Islands and Lizard Island in Far North Queensland.

It has been a journey throughout which she has faced the many challenges of navigating a very demanding industry, mostly as a single woman.

In 2022, after a lifetime of moving between countries as well as several states in Australia, Wendy settled in the Southern Highlands of New South Wales and has made it her retirement home.

Since then, she has written her first book, a memoir entitled *'Life for Rent'*.

www.ingramcontent.com/pod-product-compliance
Lightning Source LLC
Chambersburg PA
CBHW030255100526
44590CB00012B/409